THE TROUT-FLY PATTERNS
OF JOHN GODDARD

Dedication
To my grandson, Christopher Overend,
in the hope that in the not-too-distant future
he, too, may be tempted to become more involved in
the gentle art of flyfishing.

Books by John Goddard
Trout Fly Recognition (A&C Black 1966)
Trout flies of Stillwater (A&C Black 1969)
Big Fish from Saltwater (Ernest Benn 1977)
The Super Flies of Stillwater (Ernest Benn 1977)
The Trout and the Fly, with Brian Clarke (Ernest Benn 1980)
Stillwater Flies : How and when to fish them (Ernest Benn 1982)
John Goddard's Waterside Guide (Unwin Hyman 1988)
Trout Flies of Britain and Europe (A&C Black 1991)
John Goddard's Trout Fishing Techniques (A&C Black 1996)

THE TROUT-FLY
PATTERNS
OF JOHN GODDARD

JOHN GODDARD f.r.e.s.

THE LYONS PRESS
Guilford, CT 06437
www.LyonsPress.com

The Lyons Press is an imprint of The Globe Pequot Press

First published as a limited edition in Great Britain by
Creel Press, Elstead, 2003
First published as a trade edition in Great Britain by
Merlin Unwin Books, Ludlow 2004
First Lyons Press edition, 2004

The Lyons Press is an imprint of The Globe Pequot Press

10 9 8 7 6 5 4 3 2 1

Library of Congress Cataloging-in-Publication Data is available on file

ISBN 1-59228-583-X

Printed in China

CONTENTS

ACKNOWLEDGMENTS

First I must acknowledge the great debt I owe to the late Ivor Picton, who so many years ago introduced me to the wonderful world of flytying and became my first instructor. I also express my sincere gratitude to my great fishing companion of yesteryear, the late Cliff Henry, a master flydresser who helped and encouraged me to become proficient in the finer techniques needed in the new patterns I was learning to tie.

My gratitude to my old friend, Nick Lyons, for his encouraging foreword, as well as to Ted Andrews for his fine line illustrations.

I must also acknowledge the great job done by Roy Eaton, a friend of many years' standing, in the initial editing.

Finally, my great friend and publisher, Timothy Benn. It was he who first suggested and then insisted that I should write this book. Initially, I had reservations, but now that it is at last completed, I am delighted that he was so persuasive.

John Goddard
12 January, 2003

INTRODUCTION

Nick Lyons

John Goddard is a fly fisher who needs no exaggeration. He is one of the world's most supremely successful and versatile fishermen — Lefty Kreh calls him the best — and he has fished for trout from his home chalkstreams to Kenya to New Zealand to the American West, under most of the occasions trout water presents. Without this broad and diverse experience he could not possibly have become the practical and innovative fly tyer this unique book reveals.

For John's fly-tying genius proceeds from his special qualifications. He is a finely trained entomologist (and a Fellow the Royal Entomological Society); he has a scholar's knowledge of the history of fly tying — from Dame Juliana to the present; and he has intense curiosity about all the ways of trout and about the waters they inhabit. All this is coupled with his cunning and advanced skills as a fly fisher. *The Trout-Fly Patterns of John Goddard* celebrates John's prodigious skills in developing new fly patterns for trout, over a period of more than forty years, and it also offers a fascinating glimpse at the origins of his famous patterns and the logic behind their development. His flies are what I would call 'fishy', as distinct from 'arty'. They were designed with a single purpose: to gull trout. This they do. They are neither as pretty nor as unusual as the flies of some tyers I know, but if you look carefully at them, read in this book why and how they were developed, study how they solved specific problems, and — chiefly — if you fish with them, their brilliance becomes clear. They catch more fish when other flies catch only a few, and they catch some fish when no other flies will do so. This rare and unusual book suggests why.

When John began to tie flies in the mid 1950s, under the tutelage of Ivor Picton, he confesses to being 'all fingers-and-thumbs'. But as he developed his skills he also came to realise the short-comings of many of the accepted patterns, particularly when he had a chance to fish the demanding Abbot's Barton water regularly. After three or four frustrating years, he knew he would have to devise patterns of his own if he wanted to catch these difficult trout. To come close to exact imitation, he at first enlisted macrophotography — then not very advanced — but soon discarded such a direction. Size and silhouette, he realised, were far more important than exact imitation, and trout took a fly chiefly because of particular 'trigger points'. I first saw the effectiveness of this concept in Montana, before I met John, in a fly developed by Dave Whitlock and Jay Buchner, the Jay-Dave Hopper. Its trigger points are silhouette, body colour, and the crucial fact that the turkey-wing legs penetrate the surface film like those of the natural grasshopper. John has built these same principles into his flies. His close study of entomology, his acute observation of trout behaviour and their environment, and the attitude of the natural on the water, enable him to see what the imitation must be to be effective. That is the 'need' — and he then seeks the solution in form and substance. Each of the flies in this book was created in response to a perceived need; these are the flies that have survived years of hard fishing and have become part of the repertoire of fly fishers the world over. They have satisfied a need. Look at the famous Goddard Caddis, made of deer hair dyed grey and sculpted into the shape of a caddisfly, though it is solid; because it is difficult to sink it is the perfect caddis imitation for fast water and no fly shop in Colorado, Montana, or Wyoming can be found without an ample stock.

To meet the challenge of creating the most effective fly, John has done what some of the greatest fly tyers in Britain, France, and America have done in recent years: he liberally blends traditional natural furs and feathers with a wide variety of artificial materials such as Lurex, Antron, poly yarn, Krystal Flash, Plastazote, Ethafoam, and Micro-fibetts. No one anywhere had been more successful in extending the fly tyer's arsenal of materials and this blending may in itself be the single most exciting development in fly tying in several decades.

I have fished a number of times with John, often with his patterns, both on the Kennet, where he is a great master, and on a remarkable spring creek in Montana where we were both guests. I especially remember a day at what I call the 'Second Bend Pool' on that western river. John, Craig Mathews, and I had walked upstream, talking and taking turns fishing. The Second Bend Pool is best fished from a low, sitting position, and we three sat in a row, nearly touching, rotating our fishing, with the person farthest downstream casting. I had on a Mathews Sparkle Dun version of a Pale Morning Dun, size 18, and did reasonably well. But practically every cast John made, using his remarkable Suspender Midge Pupa, took a fish. Craig got a photograph of John with one of his twenty-inch browns taking the fly and my wife, Mari, later made a watercolour of the scene, which I used as the jacket illustration for my book *Spring Creek*. It was a memorable day — and I now never fish any river without half a dozen of John's Suspender Midge Pupas in my fly box.

I am not a fly tyer but for thirty-five years I have been a keen student of fly design and theory, even a fly addict with a special fascination for the minute architectonics that lead a fly to gull a trout. I use half a dozen of John's patterns regularly on the waters I fish and they are superb. His pioneering work has profoundly affected modern fly tying and has improved the success of thousands of fly fishers. This short book, filled with anecdotes and practical fly-tying wisdom, brilliantly shows why.

PREFACE

FLYDRESSING, an art or a craft — or something of each? That is a question which I have often pondered while I've been sitting at my bench tying a traditional pattern with traditional materials or a more exotic creation of my own with traditional, modern and synthetic materials, or even an exact imitation. I suspect that many other flydressers have done the same, or argued about it with their friends, and their views will doubtless have differed: some will have held it to be a traditional craft; others a pure art-form. My own view tends towards a third option: that it is a little of both.

The true history of flyfishing can be traced back to the late fifteenth century with the publication in 1496 of a book attributed to one Dame Juliana Berners, *A Treatyse of Fysshynge with an Angle*. In this now-famous book the good Prioress gave a list of but 12 artificial flies, but it is from these humble beginnings that we have arrived at the proliferation of patterns available to the present-day flyfisher. Few if any additions were made to the list for nearly two centuries. Mascall repeated it in 1590 with little variation, and early in the seventeenth century, in another book, he did so again. Clearly, little or no progress had been made with artificial patterns.

Then the latter half of the seventeenth century saw the publication of several important books on angling. The first was Isaac Walton's classic, *The Compleat Angler*, first published in 1653. This was followed by Robert Venables' *The Experienc'd Angler*. Then, in 1676, Charles Cotton published *Instructions on How to Angle for a Trout or a Grayling in a Clear Stream*, and finally, in 1681, another now-familiar title appeared, *The Angler's Vade-Mecum*, by James Chetham. The first two volumes contained only a few additions to the original list of patterns, but Cotton's book gave at least 50 new dressings, and the appendix to Chetham's book included an even longer list. Many of these old patterns, including 11 of the original 12, were still in general use in the early 1900s, although most had been modified and renamed.

But to return to my original theme, what is the distinction between 'art' and 'craft'? 'Art', perhaps, is usually associated with an original concept or creation, while 'craft' denotes a special skill taught by one person to another. I have little doubt that in its earliest few centuries, flydressing was a *craft*, handed down from father to son, or from fisherman to fisherman, since none of the books I have mentioned gave precise details of all the dressings. These could have survived over this period only through the skills and personal knowledge passed on from generation to generation. I believe that even today *basic* flydressing should be classified as a craft, as the skills needed to dress a fly can be learned only from instructional books or by attending flydressing classes.

Despite the seeming logic of this argument, I am sure many flyfishers will not agree with me. They have a case. One description of art in my dictionary is "the making of things that have form and beauty". Even non-anglers can agree that many artificial flies have both form *and* beauty, particularly the larger fully-dressed salmon flies. Thus we can make a good case for flydressing as an art, but not in its basic form, where one is simply copying the ideas of the pattern's originator. But art is also defined as "any branch of creative work", and this would certainly apply to the thousands of flydressers who, over the years, have been responsible for creating *original* patterns.

In support of this argument, I can do no better than quote from Richard Frank's *Northern Memoirs*, written in 1694: "Among the variety of your fly adventures, remember the hackle, or the fly substitute, formed without wings, and drest up with the feather of capon, pheasant, moccaw, phlimingo, paraketa or the like, and the body nothing differing in shape from the fly save only in ruffness, and indigency of wings."

Additionally, and due, I am sure, to the proliferation of new synthetic flydressing materials that have appeared over the last two decades, we have now what I would term a 'pure-art' form of flydressing practised by a relatively small number of skilled flydressers both here and abroad, particularly in the USA. These 'art' flydressers specialise in producing patterns not necessarily to be used in fishing, but to copy as closely as possible some of the natural flies, nymphs or larvae on which fish feed. These imitations are often so lifelike that it is all but impossible to tell them apart from the naturals.

I have been dressing flies for longer than I care to remember, but I can still vividly recall my introduction to the mysteries of flytying. This was in the mid–1950s when I took up flyfishing seriously. I was buying some tackle in Peek's, of Gray's Inn Road, in the City, when my attention was caught by the then manager, Ivor Picton, seated at a flytying bench. He was a gentle, kindly man, a talented flydresser and only too willing to share his knowledge with anyone who showed interest. He was tying a dry fly, and I watched in absolute fascination as he wound the hackle to complete the dressing.

Seeing my interest, he insisted on showing me how to do it. Seating me at the bench, he put a new hook in the vice, a bobbin with thread in my hand, plucked a new hackle from a cape and suggested I secure it to the hook and wind it around the shank. At first I was all fingers-and-thumbs, but after half-an-hour's tuition I was able to wind a reasonable hackle. Within a few weeks I was tying my own flies, and I shall never forget the first trout I caught on one of my own creations — an indifferent Black and Peacock Spider taken by an obviously inexperienced Blagdon brown trout. I have rarely bought a fly since that day, and the added interest and enjoyment of dressing flies and eventually developing new patterns has added a new dimension to my sport. I feel very sorry for those flyfishers who, after many years' fishing, are still buying flies rather than tying their own. They are missing out on a great deal of satisfaction gained from catching fish on flies tied by oneself.

In the late 1950s I joined the Piscatorial Society shortly before they obtained a 15-year lease on the water the great Skues fished for most of his life, the Abbots Barton water on the Itchen just above Winchester. It was my experience on this water that eventually persuaded me to develop patterns of my own. Many members eventually gave up fishing there as they found it too difficult, and after fishing trout waters all over the world, I still believe this stretch of the Itchen to be one of the most demanding and challenging waters anywhere. This is for two reasons: first, most of the water runs through open water-meadows with little or no cover; second, the water is not only gin-clear but over most of the fishery is slow-flowing, which allows the trout all the time in the world to inspect an offering. On many other chalkstreams, including the Test, the trout will often accept any old general pattern; not so at Abbots Barton. There, in the old days at least, you had to present a pattern that was a reasonable match to the hatching fly or you stood little chance of catching a fish. After three or four frustrating years on this water, I decided I would have to devise patterns of my own to fool these wary trout. First I took close-up colour transparencies of all the different species of fly to be found on the fishery. I reasoned that if I could produce life-size colour photographs, I would at least have models on which to base my fly-designs. Little did I realise how long this would take; neither did I appreciate the immense problems to be solved in producing good life-size colour images of such tiny insects.

The technique is now called macro-photography, and not only is it now well-documented, but today electronic flash and special lenses make it a relatively simple task. I had to work with extension tubes and photo-floods, and it took me nearly two years and more than a thousand exposures before I achieved results which satisfied me. Then I was disappointed to find that the resultant transparencies did not help as much as I had hoped in the development of new patterns. However, on the plus side, without them my first book, *Trout Fly Recognition*, would never have been written.

Among the patterns I eventually developed for Abbots Barton were the Cream Spinner, the Pink Spinner, the Yellow Halo, the Last Hope and the PVC Nymph. Of these, only the latter two have stood the test of time, and today they are well-known and popular patterns. In those early days, not only did I believe in matching the hatch, but I also believed it essential to produce patterns that were as close as possible to the natural insect. It wasn't until the mid-1970s, when I became involved in under-water photography, that I began to change my ideas. While I realised that our view of the trout's underwater world would never be the same as its, I did know that it would be similar. Now, my sub-surface view of the creatures on which trout feed, both at and below the surface, made me realise that exact imitation was far less important than I had thought.

Since then I have concentrated on other aspects of fly-design, rapidly concluding that, from the trout's point of view, size and silhouette are most important, while for flydressers it is simplicity of design and availability of materials that matter most.

Since the early 1980s I have also come to appreciate the probable importance of certain key points for which fish may be looking in the various species on which they feed. For example, it may be the length or even absence of tails, or the size or colour of the wings, or even the presence or colour of the eggs in the females of some species, such as in freshwater shrimps or the sedge-fly called the grannom. These I now refer to as trigger points, and I always try to incorporate them in any new fly-designs.

THE BLACK FLY

This is one of my most recent creations, which, like the following pattern, can be dressed on a small hook to represent the various species of black gnat or on a larger hook to represent the hawthorn fly.

I do not usually publicise a new pattern until it has taken at least 50 fish and had at least a full season's use. This is an exception. It has certainly not accounted for anywhere near that number of trout, but I feel it has potential. Furthermore, it is a simple pattern that can be tied very quickly.

I started using this pattern, on a size 12 hook, at the beginning of the 2000 season to represent the natural hawthorn flies which were occasionally being blown on to the water. It was a poor hawthorn season, but the fly did account for some nice browns when other rods were having little success. Later in the season, dressed on a size 16 hook to represent a black gnat, it accounted for several nice trout, including two lovely browns of more than 5lb each from a small carrier of the Test, fish which I had failed to catch on other patterns.

But why should this pattern be more effective than many of the standard dressings? When Brian Clarke and I were working on our book *The Trout & The Fly* we noticed that many natural flies, particularly terrestrial species such as the two I have mentioned, were often blown on to the water so hard that the whole of their bodies pierced the surface film. It was with this in mind that we developed a new pattern, described in the book, which we called the USD (Upside-down) Hawthorn. This fished with the hook uppermost, so that the whole of its body pierced the film. Not only did it look more natural to the fish, but it was easier for them to see. It was a killing pattern, but difficult and time-consuming to dress — which is why I developed this new pattern. Quick and simple to dress, the body of the Black Fly also pierces the film, and I believe it is this that accounts for its success. A legion of Black Gnat and Hawthorn patterns are to be had, but while most of them catch fish, they are all dressed with hackles which tend to keep the body to some extent above the surface, which makes them less effective than they might be.

The Dressing

Hook :   Wide-gape down-eyed, sizes 12 to 20.
Silk :   Black.
Hackle :   Fine coastal deerhair dyed black and tied fan-shape
              over the eye of the hook.
Body :   Black 'Antron' body wool.
Wing :   Bunch of pearl 'Lurex'.

First, tie in the half-hackle of very fine deerhair — coastal deerhair is best. Clip off a small bunch, level the fibres in a stacker, tie them in about J in from the hook-eye, and spread them over the top of the shank in a fan-shape. The deerhair can be dyed black before use or natural hair can be coloured with a black waterproof marker after being tied in.

Now tie in at the bend a length of black 'Antron' body wool and form a slightly tapered body.

Finally, tie in a bunch of pearl 'Lurex' immediately behind the hackle and over the body.

THE BLACK GNAT

Countless dressings represent the many and various species of small black flies generally termed black gnats. Some can be traced back as far as the time of Charles Cotton, and most are similar, with a basic black body and black hackle. My version is a good basic pattern, which I have used for several years, but while it is not dissimilar to most other patterns, it does have one major difference.

When developing a new pattern I do try to incorporate two important features: first, a pattern should be quick and simple to dress; and I try to include a 'trigger' point — an exaggerated aspect of the dressing which I hope will attract fish. In this pattern I felt the probable trigger point would be the wing.

If you view a natural from below, which is how the fish see it, the outstanding feature is the way in which the wings catch the attention. On a sunny day in particular the glossy, transparent wings of most species of this natural seem to reflect not only the light but all the colours of the rainbow.

One of the most innovative and well-known flydressers of the last century, J. W. Dunne, must also have noticed this feature, as he tried to give this illusion of colour by dressing the wing with a mixture of hackle-fibres dyed red and green. He did not have in the early 1920s the wide range of synthetic materials that we have today, in particular the 'Lurex', which is used in this and the previous pattern. This gives a sparkle and rainbow coloration similar to that seen on the wings of the natural.

You may ask why I use this pattern as well as the new Black Fly which to a large extent has superseded it. The answer is that I find it more effective on broken or fast water, while the new pattern seems to be more attractive to trout on calm, slower-flowing water.

The Dressing

Hook :   Wide-gape up-eyed, sizes 14 to 18.
Silk :   Black.
Body :   Black poly-yarn.
Wing :   Pearl 'Lurex'.
Hackle :   Three turns of black cock.

Tie in the body of black poly-yarn in a slightly cylindrical shape.

Tie in the wings of pearl 'Lurex' sloping back over top of body.

Take in two or three turns of a black cock hackle, short in the flue, just behind the eye.

THE BLUE-WINGED OLIVE DUN

This is one of my older patterns, perfected (to my satisfaction) after much trial and error, to represent the natural blue-winged olive dun. Of all the upwinged flies, this is without doubt the most difficult to represent with an artificial. Even those great masters of flydressing, Halford and Skues, never developed a pattern that was consistently successful, and in his latter years even Skues more or less admitted defeat and settled for an Orange Quill as the best compromise.

When I began to play around with this pattern, I was lucky to have several new materials which earlier flydressers could never have imagined, and the pattern that I evolved proved so effective on most of the chalkstreams I fished in the latter half of the season that it is the only one of my dressings I have never publicised — until now.

Mind you, it was not infallible, but it was a real winner compared to other patterns I had tried over the years. Unfortunately, it is not a pattern I use often these days, as I rarely fish into the late evening. This apart, the big hatches of this and other upwinged flies that we used to enjoy on most of our streams are now almost a feature of the past. The last five or six years have seen a great decline in hatches, and even on the Test, always noted for its large and consistent hatches of various species of olive, it is now not uncommon to spend a day and rarely see an olive of any sort.

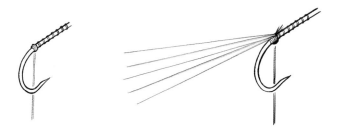

The Dressing

Hook :   Wide gaped up-eyed, sizes 12 or 14.
Silk :   Orange.
Wings :   Calf's tail dyed pale grey.
Tails :   Betts' 'Microfibetts'.
Body :   Pale-orange yarn.
Rib :   Fine gold Veniard's No 14
Hackle :   Grizzle cock short in the flue.

First, tie in the wings of calf's tail split into a V-shape with a figure-of eight tying and sloping slightly forward over the eye of the hook.

Next, tie in the tails of four or five Betts' 'Microfibetts', first forming a small ball of tying silk at the bend so that the tails flare out nicely when snugged down.

Now tie in a length of fine gold tinsel for ribbing followed by the body of pale-orange poly-yarn wound in to form a slight cylinder.

Finish with three or four turns of grizzle cock hackle tied in on either side of the wings.

The calf's tail I use on this pattern and on my equally killing Poly May Dun and Spinner is an exceptional winging material. It can be ordered through Veniard's and dyed to any colour.

THE COPPERKNOB

This is a simple nymph pattern based on the well-known and effective GRHE Gold nymph. However, unlike that pattern, which is dressed on a standard-length hook, the Copperknob is dressed on a long-shank, the reason for which I shall explain when I describe two of my later patterns also dressed with weighted heads.

I developed this pattern about five years ago initially for grayling, which seem rather attracted by a little bit of red in a dressing, but it also seemed to interest trout. During my second season with it, mainly for grayling, I invited that well-known stillwater fisher and flydresser, Tom Saville, to join me for a couple of days' grayling fishing on the upper Test. I gave him a sample or two of my new fly to try and he caught so many trout and grayling on it that it left him in no doubt as to its effectiveness.

Later that season he used the pattern on Rutland Water and it caught him so many fish that he subsequently featured it as his fly of the month in *Trout and Salmon*. I had not at that time given the fly a name, but in his column he called it The Copperknob. The name has stuck and the fly is now one of the standard nymph patterns always to be found in my fly-box.

The Dressing

Hook :   Down-eyed long-shank sizes 12 to 16. – Fulling mill
             No 31710.
Silk :   Brown.
Tag :   Bright crimson wool.
Body :   Dubbed hare's ear.
Rib :   Fine gold Veniard's No 14.
Head :   Copper bead of appropriate weight.

Slide a copper bead of the chosen size and weight round the bend of the hook and up to the eye.

At the hook-bend tie in a short length of crimson wool.

Next, tie in a length of fine gold tinsel for ribbing, followed by the dubbed hare's ear.

Finally, take the dubbed hare's ear up to the bead to form the body and then rib.

THE DAMSEL WIGGLE NYMPH

One of my earlier patterns, this was developed for fishing at Grafham Water shortly after the reservoir opened. The stream that ran through the valley, before it was flooded, hosted substantial numbers of damsel flies, and these spread rapidly along the reservoir shores as the water level rose. By the second year excellent shoreward migrations of the damsel nymphs were being seen from June onwards.

These nymphs, when ready to hatch, swim shorewards just below the surface with a distinct wriggling motion. I was using Cliff Henry's Damsel Nymph pattern, but while this is an excellent fly and brought some nice fish, I felt I could do better with a dressing that provided at least a modicum of movement similar to that of the natural. The Wiggle Nymph that I eventually perfected seemed to do the trick, and now it is my most favoured pattern on stillwater when damsels are hatching.

The fly is unweighted and should be fished just beneath the surface on a floating line. The retrieve should be fairly slow with frequent pauses, which imparts a distinct wriggle somewhat similar to the natural's. The nymphs of the blue damsel, the commonest found on most UK stillwaters, vary from olive-green to a brownish-olive. The nymphs of the red-damsel, encountered on some waters (and the commonest species on many stillwaters in New Zealand), vary from mid-brown to dark brown. Where these are found, little success will be had unless the artificials are dressed with dark-brown bodies.

While my Wiggle Nymph and other damsel patterns will take fish throughout the day from mid-June onwards, the best time to fish them is from mid-morning to early afternoon, which is when the hatch is normally at its peak. They can be fished from a boat with a modicum of success, but generally they do far better fished from the bank to represent the naturals migrating shorewards.

The Dressing

Hook :   Wide-gape down-eyed medium long-shank, sizes 10 or
              12.
Tail :   The points of three cock hackles, dyed olive.
Body tail :   Dubbed seal's fur, olive or olive mixed with brown, or
              olive 'Antron' body wool.
Rib :   Fine silver or gold Veniard's No 15.
Main body :   As for tail.
Rib :   As for tail.
Thorax :   Dark olive seal's fur or fibres from peacock eye.
Wing-case :   Three strands of turkey herl dyed brown.
Beard :   A bunch of speckled partridge fibres.

Dress the tail section first on a size 14 or 12 hook and then cut off the bend. Tie in three olive-dyed cock hackle-points spread well apart to represent the three tails. Tie in a length of fine gold No 14 ribbing at the bend.

The body of this tail section should be dubbed either with olive seal's fur or a mixture of olive and brown; or, as an alternative, olive 'Antron' body wool. Finally, rib the body.

Take the hook out of the vice and, with a haywire twist, secure a length of stainless steel trace wire of 40-60lb test to the eye. Then, with the tying thread, whip the forward section of the wire along the shank of the main body hook.

Tie in a length of fine gold No14 ribbing at the bend and then dub the body with seal's fur or body wool and rib. Form a thorax from dark-olive seal's fur and form a wing-case from three strands of brown-eyed turkey herl doubled and redoubled.

Finally form a beard from a bunch of speckled partridge fibres.

THE GERROFF

I developed this pattern during the drought of 1976, when late summer saw many rivers of southern England suffering from unprecedentedly low water. I had a rod on a lovely stretch of the upper Kennet, but by early July the water was so low that it had hardly any flow. This retarded the growth of most of the common water-plants, while promoting the growth of the dreaded silkweed.

Hatches of upwinged flies were very poor in these conditions, so fishing was mainly with nymphs. However, with little or no flow even small light-weighted nymphs sank quickly into the dense silkweed before the trout could intercept them. Unweighted nymphs brought little or no success as the trout were disinclined to come up for them, and it became apparent that what was needed was a pattern that would sink but do so extremely slowly.

After much trial and error I eventually hit on the idea of combining a largish hook with a minimum of dressing to give a very slow, but positive, sink-rate. I based the dressing loosely on the freshwater shrimp, which is prolific on most southern waters, and it proved extraordinarily effective, accounting for many large trout during the rest of that summer.

I half expected the pattern would die a natural death as the conditions for which it was devised occur so rarely on rivers. However, it soon proved itself an excellent pattern on many stillwaters, particularly the smaller fisheries where the water was clear enough to present it to cruising trout. It has since accounted for many large trout in the gin-clear lakes of New Zealand.

Why did the pattern gain such an odd name? The explanation is simple. Shortly after I perfected it I invited my old friend Brian Clarke for a day's fishing on the upper Kennet and gave him the unnamed fly to try. I suggested he walk downstream for a couple of hundred yards and fish it back up to the Hatchpool while I sat to enjoy a coffee. Quite a few small rainbows were in the river after escaping from a fish-farm upstream, and every so often I heard him shouting, "Get off!". By the time he reached me at the Hatchpool that had shortened to, "Gerroff!", and from then on that is what it was called!

The mixture of seal's fur used in the Gerroff is the same as that in my successful Mating Shrimp pattern, and I think that this has been instrumental in its success. It is also a simple dressing that can be tied quickly.

The Dressing

Hook :   Down-eyed medium/long-shank, sizes 10 to 14.
Silk :   Brown.
Back :   A strip of ³⁄₁₆in. wide opaque PVC.
Body :   Seal's fur : 50 per cent olive, 35–40 per cent pale to
             mid-brown, and 10–15 per cent fluoro pink

Tie in the strip of PVC halfway up the hook-shank.

Next, dress the body with dubbed seal's fur in the proportion specified. Mix the three colours together until they are well blended, and then cover only half the length of the hook-shank.

Finally, stretch the PVC over the top of the body, secure it at the eye and, with a dubbing needle, pick out the seal's fur beneath the body to represent legs.

THE GHOST PUPA

This recently created pattern has proved effective on many of the rivers I fish, particularly in late afternoon/early evening when sedges are hatching. I haven't yet tried it on stillwaters but I think it would be equally effective there.

I have been experimenting with various emerging or hatching sedge/caddis patterns for many years and although they have been reasonably successful, I have never been completely happy with them or any others available. The difficulty lies, I think, in reproducing in fur or feather the opaque feature of the case of the ascending or hatching pupa.

With the Ghost Pupa I think I have to some extent cracked this problem by tying very fine pale-coloured rug wool around the body instead of over. This does vaguely give the impression of the body colour underneath the pupal case.

This was an idea I had had in mind for some time, but I had been unable to find a suitable material. In fact it had been to hand for many years, but I had failed to appreciate its potential. I 'discovered' it while I was tying a popular salt-water pattern called the Gotcha. The wing of this pattern is formed from a dark cream-coloured rug wool. I had dressed half-a-dozen of these, but had tied in the wing of one too closely to the body, so that it almost overlapped it. I was wondering whether I should take the wing off and start again when I suddenly realised that I was looking at the perfect pupal case.

This wool is a very fine and supple synthetic material, and if a small bunch is tied in on the side of the body just behind the eye and then taken around the back of the body, down the other side, and tied off again just behind the eye, it forms an almost perfect pupal case.

In the completed fly the rug wool gives a rather bulky appearance, but once the fly is wet the wool shrinks and closes around the body, transforming the appearance. The pattern has accounted for some large trout, but so far I have used it only at the back-end of one season. It can be fished either in the surface or just below; or it can be dressed with some weight, allowed to sink to the bottom and then fished induced-take style. I dress it with three different body colours; orange, olive-green or grey. (The rug-wool specified is now marketed as 'Fly Fur'.)

The Dressing

Hook :   Medium/long-shank down-eyed, sizes 10 to 14.
Silk :   As body colour.
Body :   Orange, olive-green or grey polypropylene yarn.
Case :   A bunch of blonde 'Fly Fur'.
Antennae : Two or three pheasant-tail fibres.
Beard :   A bunch of speckled partridge.

Tie in the body material of the desired colour in a cylindrical shape.

Now tie in a small bunch of blonde 'Fly Fur', at the side of the body, just behind the eye, extend it around the back of the body and down the other side, and tie it off on the side just behind the eye.

Next tie in two or three pheasant-tail fibres just behind the eye and over the top of the body.

Finally, secure a bunch of speckled partridge fibres as a beard to represent the legs below the body and behind the eye.

THE GODDARD CADDIS

One of my earliest yet most successful and popular patterns, this was developed in conjunction with my late great friend and fishing companion, Cliff Henry, in the early 1960s. We were heavily into stillwater flyfishing and keen to catch more trout on the dry fly at a time when the technique was rarely practised on lakes and reservoirs. We thought our best chance of getting trout to rise to the dry fly would come from June onwards in late afternoon/evening, when hatches of sedge-flies (caddis) were at their optimum. We tried many different sedge patterns, but no matter how well we greased them, they would never float for any length of time, which was most frustrating. We needed a pattern that would overcome this problem. A new American pattern recently introduced to British flyfishers had been taking a lot of trout when fished quite fast just below the surface. Cliff had a sample or two and when he showed them to me, the little ball of deerhair spun on the hook just behind the eye started bells ringing. Knowing that deerhair was extremely buoyant, I asked Cliff if it was feasible to extend the deerhair along the body and clip it to the shape of a caddis wing. Being a gifted flydresser, he quickly produced a fly which looked promising, and after much trial and error we eventually had a pattern that incorporated a body below and a substantial hackle in front. This not only looked lifelike but floated like a cork. We fished it on stillwater on the dead drift during the day or by skating it across the surface in late evening as the light began to fade. Both methods were successful and provided us with many trout. Indeed, the fly was so successful, we could hardly believe it! Eventually, we started to fish it on rivers, where, dressed in smaller sizes, it proved equally effective.

Within a year or two the pattern had become popular with reservoir fishers as the G&H Sedge, a name formed, of course, from our joint initials. The reason I now list it under my own name is simply explained, although I had little to do with it.

In the late 1960s, or early 70s, a good flyfishing friend in America wrote to ask if I could provide two or three days' fishing on one of our chalkstreams for a friend of his who was shortly to visit the UK. This was the well-known flydresser André Puyans, who owned a tackle-shop and flydressing business supplying tackle-shops throughout the west coast of the States. I arranged with a friend to take him on a good beat of the Test. We had a few nice fish during the first day, but I was looking forward to the evening and a good hatch of sedges. The weather was kind, a fair hatch started and soon I had hooked, landed and returned four nice trout. Then André appeared, telling me he had had no luck with the sedge patterns he had in his box. As I had taken all the fish on our new pattern, I gave him half-a-dozen to try. To cut a long story short, he caught so many trout on it over the next few days that he left singing its praises.

Unfortunately, I omitted to tell him the name we had given it, and although he wrote to thank me for the wonderful fishing, what he didn't tell me was that he had decided to market the pattern under my name. I was unaware of this until I visited Montana in 1980, where I was astounded to find every tackle-shop had masses of our pattern on display in different sizes, all being sold under the name the Goddard Caddis. Over the years it has become one of the most popular patterns on many of the big, tumbling rivers of the western USA, due mainly to its incredible floatability.

I am surprised the pattern has become so popular here, because it is neither quick nor easy to dress, and spinning the deerhair on a bare hook demands considerable dexterity. I no longer bother to add the dubbed seal's fur underbody on a looped thread, as I find it easier and just as effective to colour the underbody of the deerhair in the desired shade with a waterproof marker.

The Dressing

Hook :   Long-shank down-eyed wide-gape, sizes 10 to 14.
Silk :   Strong brown.
Body wing : Formed from deerhair rolled around the hook-shank.
Hackle :   Two substantial, good-quality red cock.

Spin the deerhair tightly around the shank of a bare hook and trim it
to the desired shape with a pair of sharp scissors.

   Take two substantial brown hackles from a red cock cape and wind
four or five turns just behind the eye, leaving the trimmed stalks facing
forward to simulate the antennae of the natural sedge-fly.

THE GODDARD SMUT

Flyfishers have long been beset by the problems posed by trout feeding on tiny reed-smuts, those minute black flies often referred to as the 'Black Curse'. Trout taking them are all but impossible to catch, and this pattern is one I developed in the late 1970s in an effort to bring some success.

Even the doyen of dry-fly fishers, the great F. M. Halford, considered fish feeding on reed-smuts to be uncatchable, although in his later years he did introduce two patterns to represent them. Unfortunately for him, they were rarely successful, probably because the tiny hooks needed were then unobtainable.

My pattern was only moderately successful in its early days. It was often accepted by the trout, but it was another matter entirely actually to hook and land them. First, it was difficult to obtain a good hook-hold with such tiny hooks; second, I had to mount them on a tippet or point of 7x monofilament testing at less than 2lb breaking-strain, as thicker mono would not go through the eye of the hook. Even if I was fortunate to obtain a good hook-hold, I rarely landed trout of much more than 2lb.

The situation is different today and I now look upon this pattern and my tiny Suspender Midge Pupa patterns as sheet anchors when I come across trout feeding on tiny midge pupa or reed-smuts. The reason for the considerable success of these patterns is due to several factors. Two types of leader (tippet) material now available are much stronger and thinner than the old mono. These are 'Copolymer' and 'Fluorocarbon', and with these we can fish these tiny patterns on tippets of 4lb and even 5lb breaking strain. In addition, I now rarely fail to hook a fish on these tiny hooks if one is accepted due to a simple ploy: after I have tied the fly to the tippet, I offset the hook-point with a pair of pliers. This is amazingly effective. In fact, I now offset the hook of every dry fly I use, no matter what size.

I was introduced to this stratagem in the mid-1980s when fishing in Montana with an experienced midge-fisher, one Herbert Wellington. We were fishing tiny flies on a weedy spring creek, and while he was hooking, landing and releasing trout after trout, I was failing to hook any. I was feeling embarrassed at my lack of success, so at lunch I asked him what I was doing wrong. After asking several questions, he asked to look at the fly I was using. "That should be fine," he said, but then "Oh! You haven't offset the hook!". From then on I matched him fish for fish. Herbert also introduced me to 'Power Gum' and showed me how and where to mount a 10-12-inch length in the leader. He had perfected its use in his leader to enable him to land many double-figure trout even on his 4lb tippet. I now use 'Power Gum' in all my leaders. Not only does it allow very big fish to be landed on very light tippets, but it results in fewer flies being lost in trees and bushes on the back-cast, when they invariably break off with a normal hook.

The Dressing

Hook :   Fine-wire up-eyed, sizes 18 to 22.
Silk :   Fine black.
Body :   Two black ostrich fibres or black wool.
Hackle :   Two turns of black cock hackle, short in the flue.

This is an exceptionally simple pattern and quick to dress.

Use a hook that is very fine in the wire and for the body take two black ostrich fibres and wind them on halfway along the hook-shank to just short of the eye.

Then take two turns of a black cock hackle short in the flue just behind the eye — and that is that!

THE HATCHING
MIDGE PUPA

I developed this pattern in the early 1960s when I was deeply involved in stillwater fishing and really heavy hatches of chironomids (midges, as they are called by many flyfishers) were the norm. Some of the smaller species, and a few of the larger, would hatch during the day, but the heaviest hatches of the larger species usually occurred either early in the morning or in early evening. As they were (and still are to some extent) a major source of food for the trout, it became increasingly obvious that a more acceptable pattern than any of those then available was needed. To learn more about them, I collected various midge larvae from some of the waters I fished and set them up in an aquarium. Over a period of many months I watched them pupate and eventually migrate to the surface, where they hatched into adults in the surface film. The pupae were of particular interest, as it was their appearance and behaviour I wanted to simulate in any fly-pattern I devised.

Apart from the strongly curved and segmented body, the most interesting features (which no one had ever tried to copy in fur or feather) were the bunch of breathing filaments at the head of the pupae and the caudal fins at their tails, both of which were pale, almost white, in colour. I noticed, too, that the thorax of many species varied from dark brown to almost an orange-brown.

These were the features I now concentrated on and incorporated in my new dressing.

This pattern was certainly much more effective than any of those I had used previously, and it quickly became popular. Today, dozens of midge-pupa patterns are available, but while many have subtle variations, most still incorporate at least some of the features of my original.

The new dressing brought most success when used on a floating line in a team of three on a long leader fished sink-or-draw from the bank, or on the slowest possible retrieve from a boat. I also fished it dead drift on a greased leader on the surface to simulate the natural pupa hanging in the surface film before hatching. This method gave some success, but it was all but impossible to keep the fly floating in the film for more than a couple of minutes. Once it had sunk even an inch or so beneath the surface, it seemed to lose all appeal to the trout. Many years later I solved this particular problem with my successful Suspender Midge Pupa, which I describe later.

I still fish the Hatching Midge Pupa, but mostly during the day, as I find it much less effective once a hatch is under way in the early morning or evening, when the trout are usually close to the surface looking for the pupae hanging in the film. I dress the fly in various colours so that I can match the colour of the pupae hatching at any given time.

The Dressing

Hook :   Drennan Suspender hook, sizes 10 to 14.
Silk :   As body colour.
Tag :   Several strands of white nylon filaments projecting
            $^1/_8$ inch below the body.
Body :   'Antron' body wool in desired colour.
Rib :   Silver tinsel Veniard's No 16.
Thorax :   Three strands of turkey or peacock herl.
Head Filaments : A small bunch of white baby wool.

Starting at the eye, take the tying thread as far round the bend as possible and tie in the tails (tag).

Next, tie in a length of wide silver tinsel for the rib.

Now tie in a length of 'Antron' body wool of the chosen colour, wind it up the shank to within G inch of the eye, and rib.

Next, tie in a small tuft of white wool sloping forward over the eye of the hook.

Finally, make a rope of either brown-dyed turkey fibres or peacock herl for the thorax by twisting three strands together and wind this on behind the eye, lifting the tuft of white wool so that two strands are wound in front of it.

THE J G EMERGER

My most recent pattern, developed over the past two seasons, is similar in appearance to that excellent artificial the Klinkhåmer, which I believe is intended to represent an emerging olive dun. But my pattern is really quite different and is meant to represent the olive emerging from its shuck.

Given my belief in incorporating 'trigger points' in artificial flies, it was this aspect on which I concentrated in designing this new pattern, and the triggers in this case, I decided, were part of the shuck from which the fly was emerging and the way in which the emerging fly spread its wings apart in its struggle to gain the surface.

To represent the shuck I decided to use a relatively new material called 'Fly Fur', which in a blonde shade is used for the wing of a popular saltwater pattern called 'The Gotcha'. It is a wonderfully translucent material, and a short length tied in below the bend of the hook in my new pattern forms a most realistic part of the empty shuck.

For the second trigger, the V-shaped wings, I decided to use calf's tail dyed light grey, but this did pose a problem as when I wound the 'Parachute' hackle around the base of the wings it closed them together so that they appeared to be a single wing.

To the best of my knowledge nobody had attempted to dress a fly with such wings and a 'Parachute' hackle, so I enlisted the help of my friend John Smith, one of the UK's top flydressers. Eventually we overcame the problem by forming a short post at the base of the wings and then splitting them on top of the post with a figure-of-eight tying. Since the pattern is intended to represent the various species of emerging olive, I also included an olive-ribbed body and, initially, a grizzle hackle tied 'Parachute' style.

Now, halfway through the 2003 season, and with all the flies to be included in this book already tied, I have found that dark grey wings and a dark grey cock hackle are even more effective. The pattern has in fact proved astonishingly successful and I go so far as to say that it is the most killing dry fly I have ever designed, with an almost magical ability to pull up deep-lying trout.

Only recently I was fishing on the little River Dever with Bernard Cribbins at the back-end of the Mayfly, when the fish were sated and not rising and we had to rely on casting to fish as we located them. Although most of these were lying deep and not even on the fin, Bernard succeeded in rising, hooking and releasing seven superb trout, all 31b-plus, before lunch — all on the J G Emerger.

On another occasion I was fishing the Anton after lunch when the river was dead, with a rise nowhere to be seen. Eventually, in late afternoon, and in desperation, I decided to fish blind with my new pattern on a short stretch. Within an hour I had risen, hooked and released five excellent trout. And although the pattern was designed specifically for trout, it has proved equally successful for big grayling. It has also been fantastically successful during the evening rise.

The pattern does seem to have an astonishing ability to fool even the most educated of trout. On countless occasions over the past 40 years I have seen trout rise to a fly and then drift downstream with it 'balanced' on the end of its nose, obviously examining it closely before refusing it. When this has happened with this new pattern the fly has nearly always been confidently accepted.

This is a fairly simple and quick pattern to dress once the technique of splitting and tying-in the wings is mastered. It is also very durable. However, for it to fish properly with the V-shaped wings showing upright above the surface and the body hanging below, it is essential that it is greased correctly. Any spray flotant may be used, but I find 'Gink' the most effective. Wet the body and shuck, hold the body between finger and thumb so that no grease can reach it, and with the other finger and thumb apply 'Gink' to both wings and hackle.

The dressing

Hook:	Curved Kamasan B100, sizes 14 or 16.
Silk:	Brown.
Wing:	Calf's tail dyed dark grey and split in a V-shape. (Calf's tail is available through Veniard's.)
Shuck:	Blonde 'Fly Fur' half the length of the body.
Rib:	Fine gold Veniard's No 14.
Body:	Slim and tapered olive-green 'Antron' body wool.
Hackle:	At least six turns of dark grey cock tied 'Parachute'-style around wing root.

Tie in the blonde 'Fly Fur' for about half the body length and well round the bend of the hook, followed by the fine gold ribbing and a length of olive 'Antron' body wool.

Next, before forming the body, tie in the dark grey calf's tail by the tips about $3/16$ inch from the eye. (Tying-in by the tips helps give a nicely tapered body.) Secure the wing in the upright position and wind the thread around the base to form a post about $3/32$ inch high. Then split the wing into a V-shape on top of this post with a figure-of-eight tying.

Now form the body up to the eye, take the thread back behind the wing, rib the body with gold tinsel, and tie off.

Finally, wind at least six turns of good-quality dark grey cock hackle around the post to form the 'Parachute' hackle.

Note: Dressed with an orange-coloured body, this pattern is very effective when blue-winged olive duns are hatching.

THE LAST HOPE

It was fishing the famous Abbots Barton water of the Itchen in the early 1960s which inspired this pattern. This was, as I have mentioned in the preface to this book, the water on which the great G. E. M. Skues fished for most of his life, and it is one of the few waters I know which demands that the hatch really should be matched. I have described in the preface how research on the various species of aquatic fauna on which the trout feed eventually led to me perfecting patterns closely resembling the naturals on the water. At that time hatches of many different species proliferated throughout the season, and the fact that many of the trout tended to feed on one particular species to the exclusion of any others really did present a problem. Early in the season one of the many different species of olive that hatched was the pale watery, an extremely small fly, and when the trout were rising to these to the exclusion of similar species, they were exceedingly difficult to tempt with any of the standard patterns. Later in the season these would be replaced by an even smaller olive with a much darker body — the small dark olive — which presented the same problem.

It was in desperation that I decided to try to devise my own pattern specifically to represent these small flies, and The Last Hope was the successful result. The reason for its name was that I was then a very slow flydresser, and I would use the new pattern only when all else failed! I still use it on many of the rivers I fish, particularly when pale wateries are hatching.

The pale-bodied pattern has also proved effective when trout are rising to the dreaded caenis on both streams and stillwater.

The Last Hope is both simple and quick to dress, but it is essential to use hackles from a top-quality cape, as they should be very short in the flue. To help floatability I dress the pattern with extra long tails. I originally used three or four fibres from a blue-dun cock hackle.

Now, as for all my dry-fly and spinner patterns, I use John Betts' Microfibetts', which make superb tails and are available in a variety of colours from most fly-tackle shops.

The Dressing

Hook :   Wide-gape, up-eyed, sizes 16, 18 or 20.
Silk :   Yellow.
Tails :   Four to six long 'Microfibetts'.
Body :   Fibres from a Norwegian goose breast feather, cream
            to represent the pale watery or greyish for the small
            dark olive.
Hackle :   Three or four turns of top-quality honey-dun cock,
            short in the flue.

Take the tying silk down to the bend of the hook, form a little ball of silk and tie in four or six long 'Microfibetts' to represent the tails, snugging them up to the ball of silk so that they splay out.

Form the body from three or four fibres from a cream-coloured Norwegian goose breast feather.

Finally, wind in three or four turns of a honey-dun cock hackle.

THE MATING SHRIMP

It was a long time ago that I developed a pattern which I called The Shrimper. I was fishing a water on the middle Kennet which had not only sections of fast, deepish water, but also some deep pools. In both types of water trout could sometimes be seen grubbing in the gravel on the bottom, and it soon became apparent that they were feeding on freshwater shrimps, or cress bugs as they are known in America. While several life-like patterns were available, none carried enough weight to sink the fly quickly enough in fast or deep water, so I decided to see what I could do to remedy the matter.

The strongly-curved body of the natural shrimp obviously gave me the opportunity to include a lot of lead weight and at the same time achieve the correct body shape. I did it by using a $\frac{3}{16}$ inch-wide strip of lead cut from an old wine-bottle top and doubled, re-doubled and tiered along the top of a straight-shank hook.

The resultant pattern dressed in various sizes from 14 down to 10 (or even 8 on flies intended for the deepest pools) proved very effective for these deep-feeding trout and accounted for some really large fish. But a word of warning: when casting the larger, weighty patterns, it is essential to wait a long time on the back-cast so that the line is fully extended, otherwise a hook in the neck or ear may well be the result. This pattern was heavily ribbed and had a body of mixed brown and green seal's fur with a wide strip of PVC stretched across the top.

I used The Shrimper well into the late 1970s until I encountered a brown trout I estimated at more than 3lb (large for the water) which was lying in a deep gravel run in front of a footbridge on a small carrier, and which persistently refused every pattern I showed it over several weeks, including The Shrimper. Convinced the fish was feeding on shrimps for much of the time, I eventually collected some from downstream to examine them.

Some of them, I noticed, had an orange-red coloration, which I have since been told is connected with mating, or, as some have suggested, due to the colour of the eggs carried by the females.

I thought this a good reason to add some pink seal's fur to the other two colours in the body of The Shrimper, which did give it a reddish hue. On my next outing I crept up to the bridge and, to my astonishment, my old antagonist took my modified pattern on my very first cast! This may have been a coincidence, but I like to think otherwise, as the modified pattern, which I now call The Mating Shrimp, has since been more effective than the old pattern. Indeed, this touch of pink in the body (I now use a fluoro pink) seems to hold a fatal attraction for both trout and grayling feeding on shrimps.

The Dressing

Hook :   Medium-shank wide-gape down-eyed, sizes 10-14 (see note).
Silk :   Brown.
Rib :   Silver tinsel Veniard's No 16.
Back : $^1/_4$ inch wide strip of PVC.
Body :   Lead built up and covered with well-blended seal's fur, 50 per cent pale brown, 35-40 per cent olive, and 10-15 per cent fluoro pink.

Wrap several layers of silk along the hook-shank to form a good platform for the lead strip.

Lay the lead strip along the top of the shank and double and re-double it, ribbing each layer tightly to hold it in position, and making each successive layer a little shorter than the last until the desired shape and height have been reached.

Use a flat piece of metal to press hard against the lead to remove all the sharp edges and bind the whole of the lead body with tying thread to prevent the dubbed body slipping off when wound on.

Now tie in the G-inch wide strip of PVC at the bend with the mixture of seal's fur and rib.

Finally, stretch the PVC over the body, tie it in at the eye and, with a dubbing needle, pick out the seal's fur below the body to form legs.

NOTE : I have recently experimented in tying this pattern on one of the curved Drennan sedge hooks, which makes it easier to dress and equally effective. I use size 10 or 12 hooks and simply wrap lead wire round the shank to provide weight, which is much quicker than using layers of lead strip.

THE NEGATIVE NYMPH

"Necessity is the mother of invention." That old adage is what lies behind the creation of this pattern … A couple of seasons ago I was fishing a small local lake stocked mainly with rainbows. The water here is gin-clear and on a sunny day fish can be seen cruising from quite a distance. Many of them, stocked early in the season, grow to a good size, and by early August often run at between 3lb and 4lb, by which time they are also 'educated' and difficult to catch.

I had been fishing this water for four or five seasons and knew from experience that the few fish caught after the middle of August were those that had made a mistake. At this time of the season I tend to fish the water only in calm, bright and sunny conditions, as on cloudy days, or if the wind is sufficient to cause a ripple, the fish cannot be seen clearly enough to establish what they are doing.

During the season in question the fish at this time were unusually picky, with few rising, and I was limited to fishing nymphs. However, anything larger than size 16 was completely ignored, and if the nymph was smaller and did attract the attention of one of the larger fish, it was always refused at the last moment. Furthermore, if any movement at all was imparted to the nymph, the fish would sheer off in panic — and this was with nymphs as small as size 20.

This was most frustrating. The fish were clearly feeding, and every now and again I would see one open its mouth as it cruised along. Try as I might, I could not see what it was they were taking, so I took it to be tiny nymphs or pupae. What intrigued me was that the fish were not moving up or down, so I assumed they were feeding on something stationary or moving very slowly indeed. What was needed, I decided, was an extremely small pattern that would sink exceptionally slowly. This posed quite a problem, as even a small bare hook would sink too fast.

Eventually I solved the problem with a suspender-type pattern incorporating a small ball of 'Ethafoam' and a single turn of hackle tied 'Parachute' style.

Dressed correctly, and once wet, it has almost a negative buoyancy (hence its name) and in the few remaining weeks of that season and in the following two years it proved a resounding success, accounting for several fine bags of fish. Mind you, its use is rather restricted to those days when the weather is kind, and it is all but impossible to see it at any distance in the water. My solution to the last problem was to cast in the path of a cruising fish and then watch for any sign that the nymph had been accepted, but I have to admit that on many occasions I did strike to no avail!

The Dressing

Hook :	Wide-gape down-eyed, sizes 16 or 18.
Silk :	Brown.
Head :	A small ball of 'Ethafoam' enclosed in silk mesh and tied in behind the eye of the hook.
Rib :	Fine gold tinsel Veniard's No 14.
Body :	Olive or grey 'Antron' body wool.
Thorax :	Two fibres of peacock herl.
Hackle :	One turn of grizzle cock.

First, tie in a tiny ball of 'Ethafoam' just behind the eye of the hook, enclosing it with mesh nylon from a ladies' silk stocking and colouring it brown with a waterproof marker.

Next, dress a slim body of olive or grey 'Antron' body wool and rib.

Then tie in a small thorax of peacock herl close to the ball.

Finally, tie in a single turn of grizzle hackle 'Parachute'-style beneath the ball of 'Ethafoam'.

THE PERSUADER

Created in the late 1960s when I was regularly fishing Hanningfield Reservoir, in Essex, this pattern was developed as a general attractor to be fished when no positive indication of what the trout may be feeding on was to be had — a frequent occurrence on large waters. Hanningfield was an extremely rich water when I first started to fish there. Huge hatches of various species of chironomid (midges) were common and formed a staple diet for most of the trout. Later in the season masses of perch-fry were present, and added to these were often good hatches of damsel nymphs, so the surface fishing, especially for rainbows, was particularly good. Unfortunately, by the late 1960s the perch were more or less wiped out by disease and many of the other species declined alarmingly, to such an extent that most rods were forced to fish with sinking lines for the brown trout that seldom seemed to rise. These browns were picky and often much time was wasted trying to find out what they were feeding on, so I decided to dress a general pattern that might attract the occasional brownie so that I could spoon it to establish what it was taking. I thought a white body would appear fry-like, and to this I added an orange head, a colour which seems strangely attractive to stillwater trout. Finally I opted for a long-shank hook to give the fly a silhouette similar to that of a sedge pupa.

This pattern was a winner and quickly became established with many of the regular rods, accounting for many fine brown trout and some of the rainbows. Later it proved to be a good point-fly fished on a floating line, particularly during the latter half of the summer, when many big reservoirs suffer from algal blooms which colour the water. It has since become accepted as a good nymph pattern to be fished for cruising trout on many of the smaller stillwaters which are regularly stocked and which have become so popular.

The Dressing

Hook :   Partridge down-eyed long-shank, sizes 10 or 12.
Silk :   Orange.
Rib :   Silver tinsel Veniard's No 16.
Body :   Five or six white twisted ostrich fibres.
Thorax :   Hot-orange seal's fur.
Wing-pads : Two or three turkey fibres dyed pale brown.

Start by tying in at the bend a length of No 16 silver tinsel with which to rib the body.

Now take five or six strands of white ostrich fibres twisted together and wind them two-thirds of the way along the shank to form a substantial body, followed by the tinsel ribbing.

Next, form a substantial thorax with hot-orange seal's fur; and finally double and redouble two or three fibres of pale-brown dyed turkey fibres over the top to form wing-pads.

THE POLY CADDIS

Though not one of my outstanding patterns, this has brought me some nice trout over the years.

The popularity of any pattern is often due not only to its fish-catching ability, but also to the simplicity of the dressing and the speed with which it can be tied. The Poly Caddis earns full marks.

A new fly-dressing material known as polypropylene yarn became available in the early 1980s. It was very buoyant, came in a large range of colours, and proved ideal for the bodies of many dry flies. It is supplied in skeins of three twists, so that one, two or three of the twists may be used, depending on the body bulk needed. For example, a single strand, when wetted, makes a nice slim body, but when dressing the Poly Caddis I use one skein on the smaller-size hooks and two on the larger. It can be dressed in several ways and in several colours. The dressing I describe is the simplest form.

The Dressing

Hook :   Wide-gape down-eyed, sizes 10 to 16.
Silk :   As body colour.
Body :   Poly-yarn of chosen colour.
Wing :   Poly-yarn as body or an alternative colour.
Hackle :   Three turns of natural red cock or grizzle in front of
            the wing or palmered.

Take a skein of poly-yarn of the desired colour and tie it in at the hook-bend.

Then form a cylindrical body and, just short of the eye, double the material back over the body to form the wing.

Lastly, wind on three or four turns of hackle at the eye.

Alternatively, finish the body behind the eye and tie in a length of yarn of a different colour to form the wings; or tie in a palmered hackle over the body, starting at the bend and finishing behind the eye, and then tie in the yarn wing over the top to slope back over the body and hackle.

THE POLY MAY DUN

Developed in the early 1980s, this is one of my most successful patterns. It was designed specifically to represent *Ephemera danica* or *E. vulgata*, commonly referred to as greendrakes, the largest of all the upwinged flies found in the United Kingdom. The females, which are always larger than the males, have a wing-span approaching 2 inches. Their bodies are cream-coloured, while their transparent wings are strongly veined and have a distinct greenish tinge.

Previously I had relied on patterns such as the Shadow Mayfly, the Fore-and-aft Mayfly, Jacques' Mayfly, my own Nevamiss Mayfly or a large Grey Wulff, which was one of my favourites. However, I was never really happy with any of them as, while they all caught fish in the early days of the hatch, none of them was particularly effective later on, when the fish become really choosy.

The basic idea for the new pattern came from an old friend, that gifted flydresser Stewart Canham. He arrived on the Kennet one day during the Mayfly fortnight and showed me a new pattern with which he was having considerable success, and he gave me a few to try. Like many patterns, it was effective early on, but less so as the hatch developed. With split hairwings in the Wulff-style and a heavily-dubbed body of cream seal's fur, its two main attributes were that it floated well and was durable, and by the end of the Mayfly season that year we had given it the name The Haystack.

The following winter I decided to develop a new pattern based loosely on Stewart's Haystack, bearing in mind the floatability of his pattern and its durability, both of which I felt were important, but I would model my version on an emerger rather than the fully-developed dun with its long tails. I kept the split wings, but decided to replace the hair with calf's tail, which looked better and was more buoyant. For the body I decided on the relatively new and buoyant poly-yarn in a cream colour, and I used the tips of the calf's tail to extend beyond the end of the body to represent the shuck of the emerging dun. I completed the pattern with a black cock hackle.

The following Mayfly season I tried the pattern extensively. It floated well, was very durable, and extremely successful. However, I was not completely happy with the colour of the wings (for which I had used pale-green calf's tail) as even at a distance I could pick out my fly from the naturals as its wings were darker than theirs.

After studying the appearance of the wings of the naturals on the water, I noticed that in strong light, particularly sunlight, the wings seemed to have a golden glow. To this day I have never understood why, because at close range they do appear greenish, but eventually I tied my pattern with pale-yellow calf's tail. The following weekend I found to my delight that I had difficulty in picking out the artificial among the naturals. The trout obviously had the same problem and the pattern was phenomenally successful throughout the remainder of the Mayfly hatch, as it has been since.

The Poly May Dun is now a popular and well-known pattern, being recommended even by many professional gillies on the big Irish loughs. It is now the only pattern that I use during the Mayfly period, and it has a relatively high incidence of success even towards the end of the Mayfly hatches, when the trout become extremely selective. It is so durable that I have often caught and returned up to 30 or 40 trout before I have discarded an individual fly. It is also a simple pattern which is quickly dressed.

The Dressing

Hook :   Partridge wide-gape, sizes 10 or 12 (No GRS2A).
Silk :   Strong brown or yellow.
Shuck : Tips of the calf's tail used for the wings.
Wings : Calf's tail dyed pale gold.
Body :   Cream-coloured poly-yarn.
Hackle : Four turns of black cock, two in front and two behind the
           wings.

Take a bunch of calf's tail and tie it in well round the bend of the hook, the tips protruding for about one-third of the body-length beyond the bend to represent part of the natural's empty shuck.

Now take the calf's tail along the body and tie in behind the eye, with the butts sticking up to represent the wings. Split these with a figure-of-eight tying into a V-shape slanting slightly forward over the eye.

Next wind on a substantial body of cream poly-yarn up to and just in front of the wing-base.

Finally, tie in a hackle of black cock with two turns in front of the wings and two turns behind.

The pale-gold calf's tail can be had from Veniard's, who will dye it especially for you.

Alternatively use the new blonde Fly Fur which I now favour to represent the empty shuck.

THE POLY MAY SPINNER

When I was finally satisfied with the dressing for the Poly May Dun, I turned my attention to the spinner, deciding to use a similar dressing with minor variations. First, I replaced the shuck of the dun with long tails. I then used four long black cock hackle-fibres, but now I tend to use 'Microfibetts', which are more durable. For the body I use white poly-yarn, and for the wings I use a well-blended mixture of white and black calf's tail, again V-shaped and slanting forward over the eye of the hook.

I still use a black cock-hackle, but only three turns and much shorter in the flue, as this pattern needs to float in the surface film, not on it. I also tie in the wings in a much wider V-shape, so that when the fly lands on the water, it falls on one side or the other, so that one wing lies flat on the surface while the other is vertical. The much shorter hackle I use on this pattern also facilitates the desired tilting of one wing.

The reason for the tilting wing lies in the naturals. When the females, and a percentage of the males, die and float in the surface film, most of them drift with one wing sticking up in the air. Have a look next time you are at the waterside during a spinner fall. You will probably be amazed to see how many of them do float with one wing cocked vertically. The trout seem at times to show a preference for these, although at others they may show a preference for spinners with both wings flat on the surface.

For this reason I always carry two spinner patterns with me, my own and an excellent pattern called the Deerstalker, designed by my good friend Neil Patterson, which has its wings tied flat.

Waiting for an evening fall of Mayfly spinners can be frustrating as it depends to some extent on weather conditions, and sometimes, even in ideal conditions when the banks are lined by dancing male spinners, no fall may occur. This is usually due to poor hatches over the preceeding two or three days, so that few if any females are available to mate and so create a fall. These days, before I decide whether or not to stay on in hope of a fall of spinners, I always have a good look in the grasses, bushes and trees that normally harbour numbers of both male and female spinners. If females are conspicuous by their absence, then I assume that no mating or fall of spinners will occur that evening, and there is little point in staying on.

The Dressing

Hook :   Wide-gape down-eyed Partridge No GRS2A, sizes 10 or 12.
Silk :   Black.
Tails :   Three or four long dark cock fibres or 'Microfibetts'.
Wings :   A bunch of well-mixed black and white calf's tail tied in a V-shape and sloping well forward.
Body :   White poly-yarn.
Hackle :   Three turns of black cock short in the flue.

Tie in three or four long cock fibres or 'Microfibetts' for the tails.

Tie in a bunch of well-mixed black and white calf's tail by the tips just below the eye and split them in a wide V-shape with a figure-of-eight tying.

Now wind a substantial body of white poly-yarn up to and just over the wing roots.

Finally, tie in three turns of black cock hackle short in the flue, one turn in front of the wings and two behind.

THE POLY WESTERN DRAKE

During the late 1980s I spent a considerable time in the United States, mainly in Montana and Idaho, where I was privileged to fish some lovely streams with excellent fly hatches. Many were upwinged flies and often I saw substantial hatches of a large species which were the equivalent of our large Mayfly. Like us, the Americans refer to this species under the common name of greendrake or, in most areas, western drake. The latter name was given, I think, so as not to confuse the fly with the greendrake which is common on the eastern rivers of the USA and similar in both size and colour to our own large Mayfly. These western drakes, while large, are much smaller than our own large Mayfly and a completely different colour.

Trout feeding on these large upwinged flies were not easy to tempt, and I eventually decided that this was probably due to the local patterns I had been using, which I felt left a lot to be desired. So on my next visit I took with me some specially dressed patterns based loosely on my successful Poly May but tied in sizes and colours to match the American natural. These proved extremely killing and over the next few years brought me some extremely big trout.

The Dressing

Hook :	Wide-gape, sizes 13 or 14.
Silk :	Green.
Shuck :	Yellow or pale gold 'Krystal Flash'.
Wing :	Calf's tail dyed pale grey and tied in a V-shape sloping forward.
Body :	Olive poly-yarn.
Rib :	Fine gold tinsel (No 14).
Hackle :	The tip of a grizzle cock saddle hackle dyed green.

Tie in a small bunch of yellow or pale gold 'Krystal Flash' about one-third of the body-length to represent the part-empty shuck.

Tie in the wings of pale-grey calf's tail just behind the eye and split them into a V-shape with a figure-of eight tying sloping slightly forward over the eye of the hook.

Wind a body of olive poly-yarn to just below the eye and rib with fine gold tinsel.

Wind in four turns of hackle, two in front and two behind the wing root using a cock saddle hackle dyed green.

Again the new blonde Fly Fur can be used to represent the shuck.

THE POLY MAY EMERGER

While the Poly May Dun is a killing pattern, even it fails on occasions. These are usually towards the end of the Mayfly hatch when the trout have had a lot of rod pressure and tend to become wary of any large artificial which is presented to them. For this reason I felt the need for a more sophisticated pattern that, hopefully, would tempt them. The result after much deliberation was the Poly May Emerger, which really has filled the bill and which over the past two seasons has accounted for some grand trout which I feel I might not otherwise have caught.

Although the pattern is based loosely on the original Poly May, it has been designed to fish with most of the body below the surface, so that it appears to be an adult winged fly struggling to free itself from its shuck. Most Mayflies emerge and take to the wing quickly unless the atmosphere is damp, so feeding trout have to be alert and quick to intercept them. A fair percentage of Mayflies do have a struggle to free themselves from the nymphal shuck, and some never succeed. These we refer to as stillborn. The trout are only too well aware of this phenomenon and know that such flies are easy prey, so much so that even those wary and educated trout sometimes find them irresistible — hence this new pattern.

I decided to represent the nymphal shuck on this new pattern with a material I had only recently discovered in place of the yellow 'Krystal Flash' I use on other emerging patterns, such as the Super Grizzly Emerger or the Western Drake. This is a fine synthetic wool called 'Fly Fur' that was originally marketed to be used as the wings of a popular saltwater pattern called a Gotcha. It is now available in a range of colours, but at first it was offered only in a blonde colour specifically for Gotchas. It was this original blonde colour that I realised would create an excellent impression of the empty nymphal shuck of the

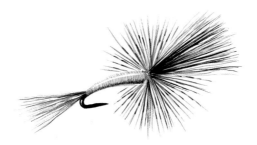

emerging fly when tied in as a tag. It is best used on larger hooks, and I still use 'Krystal Flash' on patterns dressed on small hooks, such as my Super Grizzly Emerger. This is also a fairly simple and quick pattern to dress.

The Dressing

Hook :	Curved Drennan suspender, sizes 10, 12 or even 14.
Silk :	Yellow or brown.
Shuck :	A bunch of blonde 'Fly Fur' half the length of the body. An alternative is Veniard's blonde (shrimp) Polar Fibre.
Wing :	Calf's tail dyed pale gold. A good alternative to fur for the wing is Veniard's blonde Fox Squirrel Tail.
Body :	Cream poly-yarn.
Hackle :	Black cock tied 'Parachute'-style around the wing root.

First, tie in the tag or tail to represent the shuck using a small bunch of blonde 'Fly Fur' a little more than half the length of the body.

Next, tie in a bunch of pale-gold calf's tail by the tips close to the eye for the wing, V-shaped if desired.

Now take the tying silk back to the hook-bend and tie in a fairly full body of cream-coloured poly-yarn up to the eye.

Finally, tie in a hackle of black cock 'Parachute'-style around the base of the wing.

THE POND OLIVE SPINNER

One of my older patterns, this was developed for fishing at Two Lakes, where I often fished as a guest of my late friend David Jacques. Good hatches of this fly were quite common, and on those occasions when we arrived early in the morning, we would often find good numbers of the spinners of this species lying spent or dying in the surface film, with the trout avidly feeding on them.

Unlike most other olives, these spinners do not lay their eggs immediately after mating but usually return to the shelter of trees or bushes where they remain for some time while their eggs begin to hatch into minute larvae. Then, usually during the hours of darkness, they return to the water to lay these on the surface, and then die — which is why they are encountered only early in the morning.

These spinners have a distinct apricot-coloured body, and I realised that a special dressing really was called for to represent them. They are often to be seen on ponds and lakes, and even on some of the large reservoirs, so the pattern is a useful one to include in the fly-box.

Originally I dressed the pattern with spent wings formed from pale blue-grey hackle-tips, but now I use white nylon filaments (Magic Spinner), which I find easier to tie and far more durable. I have also made a few other minor modifications, including more durable 'Microfibetts' for the tails.

The Dressing

Hook :   Up-eyed, sizes 12 to 16.
Silk :   Brown.
Tails :   Four or five 'Microfibetts'.
Rib :   Fine gold tinsel Veniard's No 14.
Body :   Pale-orange poly-yarn.
Wings :   Magic Spinner.
Hackle :   Dark honey cock hackle.

Tie in four or five 'Microfibetts' at the bend and spread them well apart by tying in a little ball of silk.

Tie in a slim body of pale-orange poly-yarn and rib with fine gold tinsel.

Now take a small bunch of white Magic Spinner winging material from Traun River Products and tie these in on top of the body with a figure-of-eight well back from the eye.

Finally, tie in a dark honey cock hackle, one turn in front of the wings and two behind, trimming off the fibres below the body so that the fly will lie well into the surface film.

THE PVC NYMPH

One of my early patterns, this was perfected in the mid-1960s when I was still fishing fairly regularly with my great friend the late Oliver Kite. Ollie was without doubt the greatest exponent of nymph fishing I have ever met, and he introduced me to many of the subtle techniques that placed him head-and-shoulders above so many others. He was largely responsible for popularising Frank Sawyer's famous Pheasant Tail Nymph, which at one time was the only nymph he used. What was good enough for the master was good enough for me, so for a long time this was the only nymph that I fished, too. It was not until after Ollie's untimely death that I encountered a situation that seemed to warrant a different pattern.

I was still a member of the Piscatorial Society when they took a lease on a new stretch of water at Axford on the upper Kennet. The water had not been fished for nearly two years, so it had a substantial head of large brown trout that had overwintered for at least two seasons and were unfortunately dark and in poor condition. Our warden rightly decided that the water would be better off without them, so all restrictions on limits were lifted for that season and rods were asked to kill and remove as many of these fish as possible.

During the early half of the season the Pheasant Tail Nymph did great execution, but as the season progressed, so the remaining trout became more and more wary and new tactics had to be considered. I was still researching for my first book, *Trout Fly Recognition*, and was collecting and photographing various fauna, including the many different species of nymph on the chalkstreams.

I had noticed that many of the common nymphs referred to as agile darters were often encountered in midwater, and these were much lighter in colour than many of the other species usually encountered on or near the river-bed. I therefore assumed that a lighter-coloured pattern might prove more acceptable than the dark-coloured PTN that the fish were now treating with so much suspicion. I noticed also that many fish would spook as soon as the artificial was moved. Normally, I start to fish a nymph on a dead drift, and then, if I have no reaction from the trout, I introduce movement for an induced take. This often proves irresistible to trout, but on a hard-fished water it can often have the reverse effect. In view of this, I decided not only on a lighter coloration, but also on a pattern that would look more lifelike, in the hope that it would be taken on the dead drift in place of the PTN that was being refused.

The conception of using copper wire to give both shape and weight to the Pheasant Tail was, of course, brilliant, so I decided to use this as the basis for my new pattern, with a pale-olive colour for the body and thorax which was lighter than the dark pheasant-tail fibres. For the tails I used golden-pheasant tippets dyed green, as these, with their dark tips, appeared really lifelike. In addition, and for the same reason, I covered the body with opaque PVC, finally adding dark wing-cases on top of the thorax like those on the mature naturals. The result was a realistic-looking nymph which, fished on the dead drift, fooled many of the trout for the remainder of that season.

For many years after I looked upon both patterns as the main flies in my armoury, depending on whether I thought the trout were taking the darker or lighter-coloured naturals. Both have now been replaced to some extent by the Gold- or Tungsten-head patterns, as these can be dressed to sink more quickly on smaller hooks. However, I still use both of my patterns dressed on small hooks (sizes 14 to 18) for fishing in shallow or heavily weeded water where a fast-sinking nymph would be impractical.

I used this pattern extensively in New Zealand, but with poor results. Then I realised that most of the natural nymphs there are dark-coloured and the PT pattern came into its own.

This pattern is simple enough to dress, but it does take a little time, and some flydressers are put off because of difficulty in obtaining the correct PVC. But this material is readily available — if you know where to look! My main source is old bathroom shower curtains, many of which were made from this material. Other plastic sheet may also do the job, but I have always kept to PVC as not only is it nicely opaque, but it has a lot of stretch and beds down well over the body material.

The Dressing

Hook :   Wide-gape down-eyed, sizes 10 to 18.
Silk :   Brown.
Tails :   Three golden-pheasant tippets dyed green.
Underbody :Copper wire.
Thorax :   Copper wire.
Overbody : Olive-green poly-yarn covered with a strip of PVC.
Wing-pads : Two or three fibres from a blackbird's wing feather.

Form the body and a good thorax with copper wire and then tie in at the bend the tails of three golden-pheasant tippets dyed green.

Now tie in a $^1/_8$-inch wide strip of PVC to cover the body and a length of olive poly-yarn for the body winding this up to the eye.

Next, take the tying thread back over the thorax, wind the PVC over the body and tie in behind the thorax.

Finally, double and redouble fibres from a blackbird's wing feather over the top of the thorax to form the wing-pads.

RED OR GREEN LARVA

I developed this pattern in the late 1960s when many of the reservoirs I fished were still having heavy hatches of chironomids (midges or buzzers) and I was keen on bank fishing as opposed to boat fishing. While this fly can be fished from an anchored boat under calm conditions, it is far more effective when fished from the bank, as it is a pattern that should be fished with little or no movement.

About 430 different species of midge are known, and many of them are found on our big lakes and reservoirs. The larvae, some of which are more than an inch long, vary in colour from olive-brown to green through to bright red. They are most commonly found on the bottom in water from 3–18 ft deep where they form tubes of mud or sand which are attached to stones, weeds or other debris, or are buried in the silt.

Some species are free-swimmers, but most attract the attention of the trout only when they leave their burrows to feed. They swim with a figure-of-eight lashing movement, which is quite impossible to imitate with an artificial. It was therefore a waste of time to retrieve the fly in a normal manner, and it was most effective when fished either static on the lake bed or with a short and slow sink-and-draw retrieve. Most takes occurred as the fly was sinking or slowly ascending.

This pattern is best fished in the afternoon, when the larvae are most active before the midge hatches of the evening. It has proved very effective over the years and brought many nice trout, particularly the red pattern, on those difficult days when little else has been hatching.

It is a simple pattern and quickly tied, but I have modified it a little using marabou instead of the red ibis quill feather, which gives the fly more life. I also use 'Antron' body wool or something similar in place of the dyed condor herl, which is now unobtainable.

The Dressing

Hook :   Long-shank down-eyed, or Drennan curved
           Suspender,
                sizes 12 or 14.
Silk :   Red or green.
Head :   Opaque pearl bead.
Tail :   Red or green marabou.
Rib :   Fine gold tinsel Veniard's No 14.
Body :   'Antron' body wool or similar of appropriate colour.

Slip a small opaque pearl-coloured bead on to the hook and slide it around the bend up to the eye as a head.

Next, tie in a bunch of marabou of the appropriate colour for the tail at the bend, and then tie in a length of fine gold tinsel.

Finally, dress the body with 'Antron' body wool of the desired colour and rib.

THE SEDGE PUPA

One of my earlier patterns, this was developed during the early 1960s when I was fishing Blagdon and Chew reservoirs fairly regularly. At the time it was difficult to find a pattern to represent the mature sedge pupa swimming to the surface to hatch into the winged fly, and I felt that if such a pattern could be formulated, it would be rewarding. I decided to 'have a go' myself to see if I could produce a reasonable likeness from photographs I had taken of several natural pupae.

This pattern was the result and, after several minor modifications, it turned out to be a killer, eventually attracting publicity as something of a breakthrough into a new aspect of stillwater flyfishing. Many other patterns have been developed since then by various respected stillwater fishers, and today we are spoiled for choice.

The pattern proved a resounding success as its popularity grew, accounting for a great many trout from stillwaters throughout the country. Today I still carry a small selection of various colours in my fly-box as a good stand-by pattern. It may not compare too favourably with many of the realistic and sophisticated patterns now available, but it does at least offer the amateur flydresser a pattern that is quick and simple to tie, with the advantage that all the materials needed will be found in even the most basic of flydresser's kits.

The pupae of many species of sedge/caddis flies found in stillwaters from June onwards are vulnerable to the depredations of trout as they swim to the surface or towards the shore ready to transpose into adults, and I soon found that the most successful methods of fishing this new pattern were either on its own on a standard tapered leader on a sinking line, retrieving it slowly with frequent pauses either in midwater or close to the bottom; or to fish it on the point of a team of three flies on a long leader just below the surface on a floating line. The first method was most successful in early afternoon, when the pupae were becoming active after emerging from their larval cases; the second was most successful in the early evening as the pupae ascended to the surface to hatch. The body colour depends on the colour of the species expected to be hatching at the time.

The Dressing

Hook :   Wide-gape long-shank down-eyed, sizes 10 or 12.
Silk :   Brown.
Rib :   Silver tinsel Veniard's No 16.
Body :   Cream, green. hot-orange or grey seal's fur.
Thorax :   Fibres from dark-brown wing feather or turkey dyed
             dark brown.
Wing-cases : Two or three pale-brown wing fibres doubled and
             redoubled.
Hackle :   Rusty hen hackle tied sparsely.

Tie in a dubbed body of seal's fur of the chosen colour on a long-shank hook and then rib.

Next, tie in the thorax of turkey wing dyed dark brown or similar fibres.

Now tie in two or three pale-coloured wing fibres doubled and redoubled to form wing-cases.

Finally, wind one-and-a-half to two turns of rusty hen hackle in front of the thorax.

THE SHRYMPH

A fairly recent pattern, this was designed to reach deep-lying trout on a stretch of the Test that I was privileged to fish. The only pattern that I had that was capable of reaching the depth needed was my large-sized Mating Shrimp, which produced some large trout particularly from deep, gravel-bottomed holes that were full of shrimps. However, I felt that in the weedy holes a nymph would be more attractive.

The problem was that building sufficient lead into a nymph to sink it deep enough resulted in a large, ungainly-looking pattern that would probably be unattractive to the trout, so I decided upon a dressing that I hoped would cover both options. This resulted in The Shrymph, which was nymph-like in silhouette but, due to the dressing, also shrimp-like. To achieve this I used the same mixture of seal's fur, with the same percentage of fluoro pink that had proved so attractive on my Mating Shrimp pattern.

This proved a winner and in the years since it has brought the downfall of some extremely big trout. In fact, on its very first outing it produced a fish I shall never forget. I was fishing the stretch of the Test I have mentioned and had just mounted this new pattern on my leader when I spotted a huge fish rise close to the bank downstream. At first, I thought it was a salmon, as the occasional one is seen on this water.

Marking the spot on the bank opposite where I had seen it move, I circled downstream to approach it from below. Once in position, I spent several minutes searching the water, but saw no sign of the fish. Then I noticed that the water where it had risen almost under the bank was very deep and furthermore the bank was undercut. After a further five minutes, with still no sign of any movement, I decided to cast the Shrymph as close as possible to the undercut to see if it attracted attention. The fly had only just started to sink when a huge head appeared from beneath the bank, the mouth opened and I was attached to what felt like a runaway locomotive.

The fish shot across the river and turned downstream with the current, and with my 5lb tippet I was powerless to hold him, so had to follow. Eventually I managed to turn him, and when he jumped for the first time I realised he was a huge rainbow. This was a powerful fish in superb condition, and provided one of the longest and most exciting battles I have experienced on a river. It took me nearly 15 minutes to subdue him, during which he jumped clear of the water at least six times and nearly weeded me twice before I was able to steer him into shallow water and jump in to lift him out. The scales thumped down to an amazing $15^1/_2$ lb plus.

The following morning I took the fish into the local fishmonger's to be smoked, and weighed on the shop's really accurate scales it still weighed just over $15^1/_4$ lb. So far as I am aware, the fish remains the largest rainbow ever taken from a British river.

The Dressing

Hook :   Wide-gape down-eyed, sizes 10 to 14.
Silk :   Brown.
Rib :   Silver tinsel Veniard's No 16.
Body :   Dubbed and well-mixed seal's fur, 50 per cent olive,
             35 per cent pale brown and 15 per cent fluoro pink.
Wing-cases : Fibres from blackbird's wing feather doubled and
             redoubled.

Wind a length of lead-wire along the hook-shank and up to the eye, and then build a substantial thorax.

Next, dub the body with well-blended seal's fur, 50 per cent olive, 35 per cent pale brown and 15 per cent fluoro pink, from the bend up to and over the thorax to the eye.

Now take the tying thread back over the thorax and tie in the rib of silver tinsel.

Finally, tie in two or three fibres from a blackbird's wing feather behind the eye and double and redouble these over the top of the thorax.

THE SUPER GRIZZLY

One of my older patterns, this was developed in the 1970s to represent many of the different species of olive to be found on many of the waters I fished.

Oliver Kite's wonderful pattern, The Imperial, was then a firm favourite of mine, and it would be accepted by most trout feeding on any of the larger upwinged flies, but it did seem less effective when the trout were taking any of the darker olives, such as the small dark olive or the medium olive, which were widespread on south of England streams, particularly the chalkstreams.

I thought it might be the light-coloured honey dun hackle that was putting off the fish, so I decided to dress a pattern similar to The Imperial but with darker hackles.

The Super Grizzly was the result. It has proved an excellent fly ever since, and it and The Imperial have served as good general patterns when any of the upwinged flies have been hatching.

Both patterns are still to be found in my fly-box, but I do now tend to favour very small flies such as The Sparkle Dun or my modification of The Super Grizzly, The Super Grizzly Emerger.

The Dressing

Hook :   Fine-wire up-eyed, sizes 12 to 16.
Silk :   Purple.
Tails :   Four or five long 'Microfibetts'.
Body :   Three or four fibres from a heron's wing feather.
Hackle :   Matching grizzle and natural red cock, short in the flue.

Tie in four or five 'Microfibetts' to represent the tails.

Now tie in a finely tapered body using three or four fibres (depending on the hook-size) from a heron's wing feather.

Finally, take three turns of good-quality matching grizzle and natural red cock hackles, short in the flue, and tie these in together.

THE SUPER GRIZZLY
EMERGER

This is the modification of the previous pattern to which I have already referred, but I fish it only on a size 18 hook. The inspiration for dressing this pattern as an emerger came about from my introduction to a new pattern called the Sparkle Dun during one of my many trips to Montana during the 1980s. I had become friendly with a well-known American flydresser, Craig Matthews, who ran a tackle shop in West Yellowstone, and I was browsing in his shop one morning when he told me that he and a fellow flytyer, John Juracek, had developed a new dry-fly they called a Sparkle Dun which was selling like hot cakes and killing a lot of fish. He gave me some and suggested I try them on the local streams. This I did over the next few days with great effect, and I came away really impressed with the pattern.

In late September, back in the UK, our trout fishing had more or less finished, so I had no chance to try the Sparkle Dun, and by the start of our next trout season I had forgotten all about it. Then, well into the season, I came across one of those 'Aunt Sallies' that refused every pattern I presented. Desperately looking through my fly-box for another fly to try, I spotted four of the Sparkle Duns I had been given. My spirits rose at the thought of trying one. They were dressed with different coloured bodies, so I chose the darkest, mounted it on my leader, and presented it to the trout, more in hope than expectation.

But not only did that stubborn fish rise, but it took confidently. Over the remainder of the season the fly accounted for several other nice trout until I lost it in a tree. The other body colours seemed less effective, so I decided to dress some for myself.

Apart from the fine deerhair for the wing, the other materials were not available here, so I had to improvise with grey heron-herl fibres for the body and pale-gold 'Krystal Flash' for the shuck. The resultant fly was as effective as the original, and lethal when any of the small olives were hatching.

It was then that I wondered whether a small Super Grizzly dressed as an emerger with the same 'Krystal Flash' to represent the partially empty shuck would also prove effective. It did, so now I had two rather similar patterns that were equally effective. Over the next year or so I found that the Super Grizzly Emerger was marginally more effective for trout, while the Sparkle Dun was marginally more effective for grayling. These are now the only two patterns I fish when any of the small olives are hatching, and both are lethal.

The Dressing

Hook :   Wide-gape up-eyed, size 18.
Silk :   Brown.
Shuck :   A bunch of pale gold 'Krystal Flash'.
Body :   Two fibres from a heron's wing feather.
Hackle :   Two matching hackles from grizzle and natural red
           cock.

Tie in the tag of pale gold 'Krystal Flash' at the bend of the hook to represent the shuck. It should be between two-thirds and three-quarters the length of the body.

Form the body from two fibres from a heron's wing feather tied in at the bend by the tips and wound to just short of the hook-eye.

Finally, tie in three turns of matched grizzle and natural red cock hackle, short in the flue and twisted together as they are tied in.

THE SUSPENDER MIDGE PUPA

One of my most successful and popular patterns, this dressing and the many modifications by other fly-dressers are now considered among the most important flies in the stillwater fisher's fly-box. When dressed on very small hooks, it is also effective on rivers.

The concept of using a small ball of buoyant material wrapped in nylon mesh must be credited to that great American flyfisher, Charles E. Brooks. His pattern was dressed as a nymph for river fishing and had the ball mounted well back from the eye of the hook. Unfortunately, the material he chose to enclose in the mesh was polypropylene yarn, which was not particularly buoyant, so the pattern was not successful and never became popular.

My good friend Neil Patterson drew my attention to this when Brian Clarke and I were developing new patterns for our book, *The Trout & The Fly*, and, being intrigued by the possibilities this concept offered, decided to explore it further.

Neil and I eventually developed a nymphal pattern using a little ball of 'Plastazote' which he found inside the outer covering of a postal envelope. We enclosed this ball in a small square of flesh-covered nylon from a ladies' stocking and then coloured it brown with a waterproof marker. We now had an excellent hatching olive pattern for river fishing that floated extremely well. All it lacked was a name. Eventually, after considering many options, we settled on 'Suspender', as suggested by Neil.

Several months later, I was dressing some of these Suspender nymphs when I inadvertently secured the ball too close to the eye of the hook, so I took the hook out of the vice and dropped it on the bench. A little later it caught my eye again and it suddenly occurred to me that although it was covered in fine flesh-coloured nylon mesh, it still appeared white, and from a distance looked similar to the white nylon filaments I use on top of my Hatching Midge Pupa pattern to simulate the white breathing filaments on top of the head of the natural.

In great excitement I rushed outside, dropped it into a glass slant-tank we were using for experiments and looked at it from below as it floated in the surface film. It floated beautifully, with the hook hanging vertically and with half of the little white ball piercing the surface. I could see no reason why the fish should not accept this for the white filaments on the head of the natural pupa. It seemed to me to solve the age-old problem of how to present a midge dressing that would float indefinitely in the surface film with the body hanging vertically below just as the naturals do. I completed the pattern by tying in a slim ribbed body and a brown thorax tied in just behind the little ball.

Over the next few months I tried the pattern on several stillwaters with flies dressed in various colours to match those of the naturals, and it was a fantastic success. Eventually I dressed the fly in a format similar to that of my Hatching Midge Pupa, and this proved even more effective.

I found the best method of fishing the pattern was to mount three in different colours on droppers 4–5ft apart on a long leader, changing any of them only if I found the trout showed preference for a particular colour. This team I fished static either from the bank or from a boat when midge pupae were hatching, giving an occasional tweak to the rod-tip to animate the flies, which often alerted a trout to their presence. During a really heavy hatch of pupae, usually on calm evenings, when the trout were head-and-tailing everywhere, the flies seemed more effective mounted closer together. Sadly, such hatches are rarely encountered today.

Many years later, when I finally appreciated the importance of small midge pupae on rivers, I found that many trout feeding high in the water on tiny flies such as smuts would often avidly accept a tiny brown or green Suspender (size 18). I found, too, that trout feeding close to the surface towards the end of an evening rise would also accept a small Suspender. This solved another problem: when fishing dry flies, particularly small patterns, late in the evening when the light has almost gone, it is often possible to make out the rise of a trout, but difficult to decide where the fly has landed in relation to it. This can be overcome by replacing a dry fly with a small Suspender, because, cast on a tight line, this makes a distinct 'plop' when it hits the surface, and this is easy to see against reflected light, even when it is nearly dark.

Another aspect to be considered when fishing a dry fly late in the evening is the avoidance of drag, so one has to fish with a slack line. In the fading light this makes it all too easy to put a trout down by striking too soon. With the Suspender this problem doesn't occur, as any drag is likely to attract the trout. This means it can be fished on a tight line and a take should be felt.

Two small modifications to the larger sizes of my Suspender Midge Pupa which I use on stillwater have increased its potential even further. I now use a Drennan curved Suspender hook, which results in a more lifelike silhouette; and I tie in a 'Parachute' hackle beneath the suspender ball, which not only makes the fly float even better and look more lifelike, but also makes it float a little higher in the water and thus easier to see at a distance. This is another problem solved, because visibility was previously a problem at times on the big reservoirs, particularly in windy conditions.

The Dressing

Hook :   Drennan Suspender hook, sizes 10 to 18.
Silk :   As body colour.
Head :   Ball of 'Plastazote' of appropriate size enclosed in white
            nylon mesh from ladies' tights.

Tail or tag :   Small bunch of white nylon filaments one quarter of
                body-length.
Rib :   Silver tinsel Veniard's No 14 or 15.
Body :   'Antron' body wool of chosen colour.
Thorax :   Brown-dyed turkey-wing fibres or peacock herl.
Hackle :   Grizzle cock hackle tied 'Parachute'-style on larger
                sizes only.

Enclose the 'Plastazote' ball in a square of nylon mesh and secure it
on top of the hook-shank close to the eye. Choose as small a ball as
possible to float the size of fly being dressed.

Next, tie in well round the bend a small bunch of white nylon
filaments and then secure a length of silver tinsel for ribbing the body
(Nos. 14 or 15 depending on the hook size).

Now tie in a length of 'Antron' body wool of the desired colour
and wind it on and secure it just short of the ball, then rib.

Follow this by tying in the brown-dyed turkey-wing feather-fibres
or peacock herl behind and under the eye to form the thorax.

Finally, tie in a grizzle cock hackle 'Parachute'-style around the base
of the ball.

SUSPENDER OLIVE EMERGER

I have been using this fairly-recently created pattern with considerable success on the chalkstreams when olives have been hatching, particularly once the sun has left the water in the early evening. Then it has often proved attractive to the trout when fished with a little movement. Drag with a dry fly is usually fatal to success on a chalkstream, but as this pattern fishes in, or partly below, the surface film, a slight but sharp lift of the rod-tip which moves the artificial but an inch or so often brings an instant response from a rising trout.

While this pattern is similar to my previous one, it is tied on a straight-shank hook and dressed as an emerging upwing pattern, and it fishes in or just below the surface film, not hanging vertically below it. The body colour does not seem to be critical, and I dress the pattern with olive-green, grey or cream-coloured ribbed bodies, perhaps favouring the last of these.

This pattern has also brought me some nice fish a little later in the season during evening hatches of BWOs, but at this time I use a fly with a pale-orange body.

The Dressing

Hook :	Wide-gape, down-eyed long-shank, size 14.
Silk :	As body colour.
Head :	Ball of 'Plastazote' enclosed in nylon mesh.
Shuck :	Blonde-coloured 'Fly Fur' or pale gold 'Krystal Flash'.
Rib :	Fine silver tinsel or brown Naples thread.
Body :	'Antron' body wool in required colour.
Thorax :	One peacock herl.
Hackle :	Grizzle cock tied 'Parachute'-style.

Enclose a very small ball of 'Plastazote' in a square of nylon mesh from a ladies' stocking and tie in on top of the hook-shank just behind the eye. Colour it brown with a waterproof marker.

Tie in as a tag at the bend a small bunch of blonde 'Fly Fur' about half the length of the body to represent the half-empty shuck of the emerging natural.

Follow this with a length of silver tinsel for ribbing and then tie in the body of 'Antron' wool in the desired colour and rib.

Now wind in a small thorax of peacock herl under the ball.

Finally, take two or three turns of grizzle hackle around the base of the ball.

THE TADPOLLY

One of my older patterns, this has been modified to such an extent that perhaps I should have renamed it. The original pattern was developed in the early 1970s when I had a rod at Littlecote on the Kennet. One of the beats included a small lake and although it was connected to the river it was only at one point, so the water had no flow. Despite this, a few good trout always seemed to be in residence, even if only temporarily.

Early in the year the lake held huge numbers of tadpoles, and trout could often be seen chasing and feeding on them. This is where the Tadpolly proved so effective, and I started to use it on other stillwaters early in the year, when I assumed the 'naturals' would be present. Eventually, I found it was also effective later in the season (probably then being taken for a leech), but only in relatively shallow water, as the original pattern was unweighted.

A few years ago I redesigned the fly using black marabou for the tail, a ribbed body, and a gold head to give it weight so that I could fish it well below the surface in deeper water. It has since proved to be one of my most productive stillwater patterns, and during the past five years it has accounted for some huge bags of large trout, particularly rainbows.

The first year after I modified it I was fishing Blagdon in late autumn with my friend Sir Geoffrey Clarkson. We had been drift-fishing loch-style all morning, using different patterns, but to no avail. Then, after lunch, we joined a dozen boats at the dam end, but fared no better. After some time, having seen not one trout caught by any of the boats, we more or less decided to accept that it was one of those dour days often experienced on stillwaters, but in desperation I decided to have a last try with one of my newly modified Tadpolly patterns. Bingo! In the next three drifts I caught three lovely rainbows, all 3lb-plus.

By this time Geoff was asking what the magic fly was, so I gave him one. Within two hours, we each had our limit of eight trout, most of them 3lb-plus. We were absolutely delighted!

I always fish the Tadpolly on its own on the point and have found that the most effective way of fishing it to be with a medium-fast retrieve with frequent long stops. The movement of the retrieve seems to attract the trout, which then approach and take it either as it is sinking or as it is rising when the retrieve is resumed. I dress the pattern on long-shank hooks in sizes from 14 down to 8, and I control the depth at which it fishes by the size and weight of the bead. I nearly always fish it on a floating line with a very long leader. It is an easy pattern to dress.

The Dressing

Hook :   Long-shank down-eyed wide-gape, sizes 14 to 8.
Silk :   Black.
Head :   Brass bead of desired size and weight.
Rib :   Fine gold tinsel Veniard's No 16.
Body :   Black wool or poly-yarn.

First, thread a gold bead around the bend of the hook and up to the eye.

At the bend tie in a good tail of black marabou.

Now secure a length of gold tinsel for ribbing and tie in a substantial body of black wool or poly-yarn.

Finally, rib the body with gold tinsel.

THE HACKLED TADPOLLY

I was motivated to tie this recent innovation when I noticed that the original Tadpolly was sometimes taken on the drop with little or no movement. This was often on hard-fished waters where trout became wary of any large patterns retrieved quickly, and it made me wonder whether the pattern might be more effective at times if fished with little or no movement while sinking more slowly in front of a cruising trout.

Initially I dispensed with the bead-head and added three or four turns of a grizzle hackle behind the eye, but then the fly tended to float on the surface for too long before starting to sink. After much trial and error I found I could achieve the desired effect by using the smallest gold bead and tying in the hackle behind it. This gave me a fly that would sink, but very slowly.

The first time I used the modified pattern it took six nice rainbows in quick succession, with most of them taking just below the surface as the fly was beginning to sink. I thought I had spooked the sixth fish as the fly landed barely 2ft in front of him, but to my amazement he simply opened his mouth and took it in as it started to sink.

I have had several good sessions with the pattern, but it is not infallible, and on occasions it has been largely ignored. However, I have at times taken a fish by imparting a little movement to attract attention.

TUNGSTEN HARE'S EAR

Gold-head patterns have become extremely popular in recent years. They originated in Europe and were, I believe, the brainchild of a well-known Dutch flydresser who wanted to give a fly some weight. He did this by sliding a metal bead around the bend of the hook and up to the eye to provide weight, and to give a little bit of sparkle to the fly, to add to its appeal, he used a brass bead. His idea was quickly taken up by others and flies so tied became universally known as Gold-heads.

The original pattern was, I think, intended to represent a sedge pupa, as it was tied on a short-shank hook, dressed with a plump, pale-brown body and called a Gold-head Pupa. It became popular in this country, but was eventually modified slightly and given a slimmer body of hare's ear ribbed with gold tinsel rather like the old Gold-ribbed Hare's Ear. This Gold-head GRHE was a really killing fly and soon became extremely popular.

I started fishing this modified pattern in the mid 1990s, but I couldn't help wondering why it was so attractive to the trout. It certainly looked nothing like a nymph, and with its slimmer body of dubbed hare's ear it didn't look much like a pupa either. I eventually concluded that it was more like a sedge larva, although the body was really too short. This gave me an idea, and I set to to tie some on long-shank hooks, which certainly gave them a more lifelike appearance. The trout seemed of the same opinion, for the new version was certainly more lethal than the original pattern. After that, I dressed all my Gold/Copper-heads on long-shank hooks, but then, a little over twelve months ago, I was introduced to tungsten beads.

I was fishing in New Zealand with one of my great buddies, Ron Clark, and as my long-shank Gold-heads had proved so lethal there the previous year, I advised him to bring plenty with him, which turned out to be fortunate.

One day we were fishing the Tekapo river, in the South Island, and I had just spent an hour casting to a large brown trout feeding avidly on nymphs just below the surface in very fast water on the lip of a deep pool. I had started fishing with small nymphs, including Gold-heads, but he would not rise to them, so I worked up to much larger weighted nymphs, including Gold-heads. Although he was initially attracted to these, he eventually refused even to look at them. What I needed, I thought, was a small but very heavy pattern, which I did not have.

Just then Ron appeared, and more in hope than expectation I asked him if he had any heavy patterns. To my surprise, he handed me a tiny Bead-head dressed with a pale-brown dubbed body on a long-shank hook. While the fly looked like one of my long-shank Gold-heads, the bead was black. It was, he told me, tungsten, and it sank like a stone. Indeed it did, and on the third cast the trout took it confidently, and, after a grand fight, was landed and weighed in at 6 $^3/_4$ lb — the best fish of the week. That little nymph was to account for four more big browns between 6lb and 8lb before we returned to the UK.

This new pattern has also accounted for my largest 'wild' brownie from a UK river. This was a fish of just over 7lb from the Test at Chilbolton at the end of June 2001, and it was 10 oz heavier than my previous best taken from the Kennet in 1986. The fly has also accounted for my heaviest bag of big grayling. This was taken over two days on a small chalkstream in August 2001, and included seven fish of 2lb or more — 2lb, 2lb 2oz, 2lb 4oz, 2lb 6oz, 2lb 10oz, 3lb and 3lb 8oz. The last is the heaviest grayling I have ever caught in this country and as I felt it to be the fish of a lifetime I decided, albeit reluctantly, to despatch it as I felt it worthy of a glass case.

I tie this pattern on a size 16 long-shank hook mounted with a 2mm black tungsten bead and dress it with a GRHE body. I also tie it on a size 14 hook with a 3mm bead. Its big advantage is that it allows a very small nymph to be fished well down in deep or fast water. I still use my long-shank Gold- or Copper-head in shallower or slower-flowing water.

The Dressing

Hook :   Long-shank wide-gape down-eyed, sizes 14 or 16.
Silk :   Brown.
Head :   2mm or 3mm black tungsten bead according to hook-size.
Rib :   Fine gold tinsel Veniard's No 14.
Body :   Dubbed hare's ear.

Using a size 14 or 16 wide-gape hook thread a 2mm black tungsten bead up to the eye.

At the bend, tie in gold tinsel for ribbing and then dub hare's ear for the body along the shank up to the bead.

Finally rib the tinsel up to the bead.

TUNGSTEN GLISTER GREEN

This is really a modification of my Tungsten-head Hare's Ear also tied on a long-shank hook which I created three years ago after I was given a new fly-dressing material that had come on to the market — Veniard's 'Glister Sparkle Dubbing'. It was a gold-olive colour and looked attractive, so I decided to try dubbing it sparingly on top of the body of one of my Tungsten-head Hare's Ears. The result seemed appealing and the trout plainly agreed. Indeed, it seemed to be possibly more attractive to them than the Hare's Ear itself. It has had a place in my fly-box ever since.

The following summer I had John Morton, a friend from New Zealand, to fish with me for a few days. He is one of the top flydressers in his country, and I had arranged fishing for him on the Test and Itchen, Blagdon and Chew. But first I took him to one of our local small trout ponds. It was a wet, windy and rather cold morning, and after tackling up he asked me what fly he should try. I decided to give him one of my new Tungsten-head Glisters, and he went on to catch and return six nice rainbows.

He was so impressed that he would use no other nymph on any of the other waters we fished over the following eight days, and at the end of his visit he estimated that he had taken more than fifty trout on it, insisting that I tie some up for him to take back to New Zealand. Towards the end of their season, he wrote to say it was proving most successful and that all his friends were now also fishing with it.

Since then I have modified it again, but only slightly. I now dress it with one of the new tungsten silver beads instead of the standard brass bead, and it seems even more effective. Towards the end of last season, in August, I had a day's grayling fishing on a small chalkstream. It was a day I shall never forget.

The grayling were few and far between and my total for the day was only eight, but four of these were more than 2lb each, and all took the new Tungsten Glister Green. So far as I am concerned, these new tungsten beads have revolutionised nymph fishing, as they enable patterns dressed on tiny hooks to sink quickly even in very fast water.

The Dressing

Hook :   Wide-gape long-shank down-eyed, sizes 12 to 16.
Silk :   Brown.
Head :   2mm or 3mm tungsten silver bead according to hook size.
Rib :   Fine gold tinsel Veniard's No 14.
Body :   Dubbed hare's ear.
Overbody : Glister gold olive.

Thread the tungsten bead up to the eye.

At the bend, tie in gold tinsel for ribbing and then dub hare's ear for the body along the shank up to the bead.

Rib the tinsel up to the bead and finally cover the body sparsely with wide spaced turns of the Glister material.

THE UPSIDE-DOWN (USD) PARADUN

Together with the following spinner pattern, this was developed by Brian Clarke and myself and launched in our book *The Trout & The Fly*, published in 1980. At the time it was a revolutionary pattern as it was the first time a fly had been specifically designed to hold its body above the surface, clear of the film, and at the same time reproduce with a 'Parachute' hackle the indentations of the feet of the natural fly in the surface mirror. Its other unique feature was that it fished upside down, with the hook uppermost — hence its name. It was never our intention to design a fly that fished with the hook above the surface, but this proved necessary to achieve our aim.

Most flyfishers are now aware that when trout are feeding at the surface on newly-hatched upwinged flies, the first indication the fish have of an approaching fly are the little sparkles of light made in the mirror by the indentations of the insect's feet, as apart from the large Mayflies (greendrakes), flies' bodies are held clear of the surface and do not pierce it and show through the mirror. Our new pattern seemed to mimic this to perfection and achieved some spectacular results during its first season, including the downfall of several 'Aunt Sallies' which for several months had defied all efforts to fool them.

However, despite its apparent potential, the pattern never proved popular, due, I think, to the fact that it is a difficult and time-consuming fly to tie. Furthermore, it demands the use of a gallows tool (which few flydressers have) to tie in the Parachute hackle. Because of this, a couple of years ago I decided to see if I could modify and simplify the pattern, and dispense with the gallows tool. This I have done, and I am delighted with the results, particularly with the split hairwings which are more durable and easier to dress than the original hacklefeather wings.

The Dressing

Hook :   Wide-gape down-eyed, sizes 12 to 16.
Silk :   To match body colour.
Wing :   A bunch of calf's tail dyed grey and split into a V
              sloping over the eye.
Tails :   A bunch of 'Microfibetts'.
Body :   'Antron' body wool of desired colour or heron-wing
              fibres.
Hackle :   Three or four turns of grizzle cock round the V-shaped
              post.

Bend a length of 30lb or 40lb stainless steel trace wire into a right-
angle to form a post or into a V-shape and cut it so that each side of
the V is about a $^1/_4$ inch long. Tie in the apex of this on top of the
hook-shank about $^1/_8$ inch from the eye. Then turn the hook upside
down in the vice so that the shank is below the hook point and secure
a bunch of calf's tail dyed grey just behind the eye and split it into a
V shape facing forward over the eye to form the wings.

   Turn the hook again in the vice so that the wing is facing down and
tie in a bunch of about half-a-dozen 'Microfibetts' to form tails well
around the bend of the hook.

   Now dress the body. I use natural grey heron-wing fibres to represent
most of the olive species, while 'Antron' body wool in other colours
can be used to represent other species.

   Finally, tie in the 'Parachute' hackle around the V-shaped post which
can now be cut off with wire-cutters as close to the hackle as possible.

THE USD POLYSPINNER

Developed alongside our new Paradun, this, too, was launched in *The Trout and The Fly* and was an immediate success. It is another pattern which is time-consuming to dress and needs the use of a gallows tool, so, like the other pattern, it has never become widely popular.

The main features of these new spinner patterns are that they are dressed on keel hooks, so that they land upside down, and they have wings specially prepared from polythene sheet which is cut into shape and pierced in many places to give an uneven surface which causes the wings to emit a pattern of light similar to that created by the veins in the wings of the natural spinners when seen from underwater.

These wings are formed from thin, flat, clear polythene sheet folded and cut to shape with wing-cutters. They are then opened out, placed on a piece of wood, and each wing pierced all over with a thick sharp needle. Done correctly, the point barely passes through the wing, but forms a distinct pimple. Wings need to be cut on the small side. If too large they spin the fly in the air and twist the leader. Anyone prepared to devote time to dressing this fly will find it a killing pattern.

The Dressing

Hook :	Keel hook, sizes 12 to 16.
Silk :	As body colour.
Tails :	Bunch of 'Microfibetts'.
Body :	'Antron' body wool of desired colour.
Hackle :	Two or three turns of cock hackle of the chosen colour.
Wings :	Formed from flat, thin, clear polythene.
Rib :	Fine silver tinsel if required.

With the keel of the hook uppermost, tie in a bunch of 'Microfibetts' at the bend for the tails.

Reverse the hook in the vice and dub the body with 'Antron' body wool to just cover the flat part of the keel.

Tie in a loop of nylon at the start of the flat section of the keel to act as a post for the 'Parachute' hackle, which is then tied in by the stripped butt as close as possible to the base of the loop.

Connect the gallows tool to the loop and wind the two or three turns of the hackle around the base. Now take the cut and prepared polywings, pass them through the loop and pull tight down on to the top of the wings and hackle.

Finally, cement them in place with a spot of glue.

The
TROUT FLY
PATTERNS *of*
JOHN GODDARD

COLOUR PLATES

This big brown trout was taken on one of my newest patterns, the Black Fly.

The Black Fly (see page 22), a pattern designed to fish 'in the film' and which represents the hawthorn fly, or any similar large, dark-coloured natural fly.

Dr Tony Hayter applies maximum pressure to hold a wild brown trout which took my Black Gnat pattern on the river Dever.

The Black Gnat (see page 24), a wonderful stand-by pattern which can be used at pretty well any time of the season.

The Blue-winged Olive Dun (see page 26). This is now the only pattern I use when BWOs are hatching. The only exception to this rule of mine is when I occasionally use the JG Emerger (also dressed with an orange body) which can be particularly successful on hard-fished waters.

A big brown is returned by my old friend Bernard Cribbins. The Blue-winged Olive was the fly for this particular moment.

A large grayling is played out on the river Test. It fell for my Last Hope pattern (pictured below) – a great fly when fish are being shy and pernickety.

The Last Hope (see page 47). Dressed on a size 18 wide gape hook, this is one of my earliest patterns but it still remains a great little fly for when the pale wateries are hatching.

The Damsel Wiggle Nymph (see page 30). A very effective stillwater pattern when damsel flies are hatching.

The Gerroff (see page 32) was originally designed for use on clear, slow flowing rivers, but it can also be a killing pattern when retrieved very slowly with a greased leader on stillwaters.

The Ghost Pupa (see page 34). A useful hatching sedge pattern which can be fished sub-surface on both rivers and stillwaters.

My old friend and co-author of our book *The Trout & The Fly*, Brian Clarke, with a superb brown trout of over six pounds, taken on my Gerroff pattern from the little river Dever.

The Goddard Caddis (see page 36). One of my most popular patterns for fast-flowing rivers, or for use as a wake fly on stillwaters.

The Goddard Smut (see page 39). One of the very few patterns available which has proved to be very effective for those difficult 'smutting' trout.

The author with a superb brook trout of 5¼ lbs taken from the river Test on a Goddard Caddis in August 1995. To date this remains the largest brook trout taken from a river in the UK.

The Hatching Midge Pupa (see page 41). One of my earliest stillwater patterns, it was the forerunner of the many pupa patterns available today and it is still a very effective fly.

On its day the new JG Emerger has proved highly effective for chalkstream trout. I now consider it to be my most killing pattern when medium or large upwinged flies are hatching.

The JG Emerger (see page 44). This is my latest pattern and it has produced some spectacular results when trout are taking the emerging flies.

A lovely brown trout from the river Test is returned by the author. It succumbed to his JG Emerger pattern.

Tom Saville playing a big grayling which took a Copperknob. At the time of this photo my pattern had no name. Tom named it after it gave him some great days of grayling fishing, and also trout fishing on Rutland Water.

The Copperknob is a superb grayling pattern, particularly when dressed on small long-shanked hooks (sizes 14 or 16). It has also proved very successful for trout.

This is one of my biggest grayling to date, a beautiful specimen of 3¼lbs, taken on a small southern chalkstream on a size 16 Mating Shrimp pattern.

The Mating Shrimp (see page 49). A wonderful pattern in small sizes for trout or grayling feeding on freshwater shrimps (cress bugs). It is also a deadly fly when heavily weighted in large sizes for big trout lying in deep water.

The Negative Nymph (see page 52). Fished on the dead drift on a greased leader on small clear stillwaters, it has proved very effective in taking those wary trout that are easily spooked by any movement of the fly.

The Persuader (see page 54) is a good general-purpose attractor pattern for stillwaters when retrieved slowly and well below the surface.

Bernard Cribbins, the well-known actor, plays a big rainbow on the river Test. This one was seduced by the Poly Caddis.

Two versions of the Poly Caddis (see page 56). Simple and quick to tie, yet very effective when sedges (caddis) flies are hatching and skidding around.

Top American angler, Lefty Kreh, casting a Poly May Dun to a big rainbow trout on the Derbyshire Dove.

The Poly May Dun (see page 58) has become a popular pattern with trout anglers throughout the world. It represents the large mayfly (the greendrake) and is much used on the great lakes of Ireland.

The Poly May Spinner (see page 61) is another useful pattern for "duffer's fort-night". I promise that you will never need any other artificial pattern for those times when spent mayfly spinners are drifting down on the surface.

My great American friend, Lefty Kreh, about to release a perfectly-marked wild brown trout (a greenback) back into the Kennet. This one took a Poly May Spinner.

I tied the Poly Western Drake (see page 63) to represent the large upwinged duns of the mayfly (the greendrakes) found on many rivers on the western side of the USA.

The Poly May Emerger (see page 65), with its sunken body, will take trout on days when they seem shy of the dun imitations on the surface.

The Pond Olive Spinner (above left and page 67), an imitative pattern for use on stillwaters either early morning or very late evening. The PVC Nymph (above right and page 69) is a lethal pattern when olive duns are hatching, both on river and stillwater.

The Green Larva (see page 72) was a pattern I developed in the 1960s in response to the huge chironimid, or midge, hatches on reservoirs. There are about 430 different species of midge, so this pattern can be tied in many sizes and in colours ranging from green to brown to red (see Red Larva opposite).

This well-conditioned rainbow, taken from a small stillwater, fell for the Red Larva pattern, fished deep and slow.

The Red Larva (see page 72), a reliable bloodworm pattern which you can confidently use on stillwaters for most of the season. You should fish it static or tweaked very slowly, close to the bottom of the lake.

The author displays a fine brown trout of over 11 lbs taken on the Sedge Pupa from the lower reaches of the famous Tongariro river in New Zealand.

The Sedge Pupa (see page 74) represents caddis flies hatching and swimming to the surface. It was one of my earliest designs when few other sedge patterns were known, but it is still very effective and can catch big fish.

The author with a fine rainbow weighing 15¹/₄ lbs. It was taken on the Test and fell to a Shrymph pattern. It may well be the largest rainbow trout ever taken from a UK river.

The Shrymph (see page 76) was developed as a versatile nymph to represent a wide range of aquatic fauna.

The Super Grizzly (see page 79) was designed to represent broadly many of the different kinds of olive dun which can be observed on rivers.

The Super Grizzly Emerger (see page 81) is my favourite pattern when small olive duns are hatching on the river. Over the years it has accounted for many hundreds of trout and grayling.

This grayling was taken on the Super Grizzly Emerger, tied on a size 18 hook.

This fine grayling weighing nearly 2½ lbs fell for a tiny Suspender Midge Pupa. This small, partially submerged fly is often more tempting to grayling than the high riding dry fly.

The tiny olive Suspender Midge Pupa (above left, see page 83) tied on a size 18 hook, is a great pattern when trout or grayling are 'smutting', or taking small surface flies on the river. The Suspender Midge Pupa, which can be tied in many colours, in sizes 12 and 14, also revolutionised midge fishing on stillwaters in the 1980s. It is now popular worldwide.

The Suspender Olive Emerger (see page 87) should be fished in or just below the surface film. I have found it a useful pattern on hard-fished rivers when olive duns are hatching.

The Hackled Tadpolly (see page 91) is the hackled version of my original Tadpolly (see page 89). The original was a tadpole imitation, but I have found the hackled variation highly effective when fished very slowly in front of cruising trout in clear stillwaters.

A beautifully spotted brown trout comes to the net. Trout like this are often reluctant to rise to surface flies during the day and this is when the Tungsten Hare's Ear is a fly well worth trying.

The Tungsten Hare's Ear (see page 92) should be dressed on a small size 16 or 14 long shank hook. It is a deadly pattern when the caddis pupae are on the trout's menu.

This beautiful grayling, showing its many subtle hues, was taken on a tributary of the river Test. It found the charms of my Tungsten Glister Green Nymph quite irresistible!

The Tungsten Glister Green Nymph (see page 95) is a modification of the Tungsten Hare's Ear which trout seem to love. For me it has proved particularly successful for the big New Zealand river trout.

Mike Weaver plays a large brown trout on the upper Test taken on a Tungsten Hare's Ear Nymph.

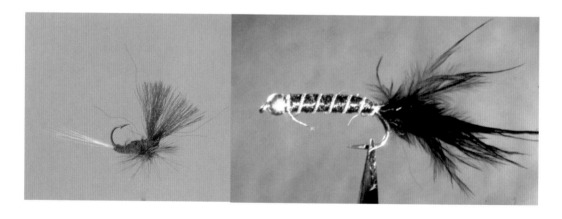

The USD Paradun (above left and page 97) was designed to fish high on the surface film. The particular tying of the hackle mimics the 'foot' indentations of upwinged flies as they drift downstream on the surface mirror. The Tadpolly (above right and page 89) is a wonderful still water pattern throughout the season but particularly effective when tadpoles are in evidence.

My fishing buddy Max King returns a superb wild brown trout of nearly 4lbs which he caught on one of my USD Poly Spinners.

The USD Poly Spinner (see page 99). Be sure not to cut the polythene wings too large or it will spin when cast and twist your leader.

This huge wild brownie, weighing 10½lbs, is about to be returned to its home in the gin-clear water of a New Zealand wilderness river. It took a lot of patient stalking but it eventually fell to a size 18 Super Grizzly Emerger.

I caught this beautiful wild brown trout of about 2 lbs on a tiny Tungsten Hare's Ear Nymph. It was on the pretty Hampshire Bourne (a river made famous by Harry Plunkett Greene's *Where the Bright Waters Meet*) and as I recall, was my only fish that day.

A big brown trout from the Kola Penninsula taken by the author on the Goddard Caddis. Trout on these Russian rivers fight like no others on earth!

Top New Zealand guide and great friend, Alan Simmons, displays an unusually light-coloured brown trout of about 10 lbs which I took from Lake Wykarmoana in the North Island on a Damsel Nymph.

A huge male brown trout weighing 12½ lbs is about to be returned. This one took a Tadpolly and is pictured on Lake Otamangakau in North Island, New Zealand.

INDEX